FIVE STAR CUISINE...at Home!

How to Make Amazing Restaurant Recipes at Home...Simply and Easily!

Bob and Ellen Rubenstein

Photographs by Ellen Rubenstein

Ellen Rubenstein

ISBN: 1-4392-5305-6

ISBN-13: 9781439253052

Library of Congress Control Number: 2009907995

Visit www.booksurge.com to order additional copies.

Why This Cookbook?

Five Star Cuisine…at Home!
A new cookbook unlike any other cookbook! This cookbook makes it easy to recreate amazing dishes inspired by some of the world's best restaurants *at home…simply, and easily!*

This cookbook focuses on incredibly flavorful dishes made from fresh, locally available ingredients, dishes that chefs, non-chefs, and weekend foodies can prepare quickly! No spending hours and hours in the kitchen! Many of our recipes can be made in less than 30 minutes. Easy to follow instructions speed along the process.

Why search the internet to decide between 1000's of recipes that may turn out to be very disappointing? Instead, go directly to a recipe that you *know* will turn out perfectly! Full color photos make it easy to see at a glance what the finished dish will look like.

No other cookbook gives you direct access to the Chefs
When you buy our cookbook you will get a private e-mail address giving you direct access to Chef Bob and Chef Ellen for prompt answers on any question you might have about any recipe or ingredient in our book.
(See page 128 *Helpful Hints from Our Kitchen to Yours.*)

We are all looking for ways to stretch our dollars in this economy and this book was written with that thought in mind. Enjoy Five Star Cuisine at One Star prices! Many of our dishes cost much less to make than buying prepared foods from the take-out deli or frozen food section in your supermarket.

Enjoy amazing food and still lose weight! Every recipe includes calorie counts per serving. Calories do count, but you can still enjoy great food even when you are watching your weight.

Chef Ellen Shopping for Dinner!

Contents

Introduction

This book was born on a trip to Europe nearly 30 years ago!
We are passionate about travel and really enjoy dining at exceptional restaurants. When we return home from a trip, we can't wait to whip into the kitchen to recreate fabulous newly discovered dishes in our own kitchen.

The problem? How to recreate these recipes at home?
For years we looked for cookbooks that would tell us how to make great restaurant recipes at home simply and easily, but no luck! The recipes were too complicated for most home chefs to tackle or would take hours and hours to prep. Many included hard-to-find ingredients or were too costly to make in today's economy.

The solution! Let's write a new kind of cookbook!
A cookbook that would make extraordinary recipes simple, easy and fun for the home chef to make! After years of traveling, researching, and dining at truly amazing restaurants and bistros in the USA and Europe, we *have written a cookbook unlike any other cookbook!*
A cookbook that will make certain that every recipe turns out perfectly.
A cookbook that gives you access to us so we can promptly answer any question you have about any recipe or ingredient in the book.

We traveled and talked, tasted and talked, jotted notes and talked. We decided to eat only at the tiny bistros and casual brasseries in France and only at the neighborhood trattorias in Italy. We said NO to 3 star Michelin restaurants and sought out the restaurants where the locals eat.

In the USA we traveled many times to New York, Boston, Atlanta, Chicago, Denver, Dallas, Houston, New Orleans, Los Angeles, San Francisco, Seattle, and Portland, Oregon. We asked friends for their favorite restaurants and, of course, referred to our handy Zagat guide. We developed our list of *must-go-backs* in each city and culinary region, taking notes about every dish we ordered, what was in it, how it was made, and how it was served.

After years of traveling and experiencing truly amazing restaurants, bistros, cafes and trattorias, we *had* to write this book!

Our search for great recipes started in Paris, where we couldn't believe the absolutely superb recipes served to us. We loved the traditional family dishes, classic regional dishes, and grandmère's special recipes, all charmingly served by delightful servers and often even the chef.

Our journey continued through the Burgundy region, the wine towns of Dijon, Beaune and Macon. Then we went on to Venice, Florence and the hill towns of Tuscany, where we were captivated by the flavors, herbs and wines of each region.

To create this unique cookbook, we developed 3 requirements:

1 *Each and every recipe must be personally tested and tasted by us.* We wanted to maintain the integrity of each dish so that it would be every bit as delicious as the original recipe. Once we were satisfied with each recipe we sent the recipe to our panel of testers. They prepared the recipe themselves to test for the ease and clarity of our instructions. Then they served the dish to their family and friends and reported the results to us.
Everyone had to *LOVE* it to earn a place in our book!

2 *Each recipe must be SIMPLE AND EASY to make,* and, whenever possible, have a color photo to show how it looks when ready to serve.

#3 *Each recipe must tell the NUMBER OF CALORIES per serving* so home chefs and their families can enjoy fabulous food like this and stay within their calorie goals.

GREAT COOKING AT HOME MADE SIMPLE…THAT'S WHAT THIS BOOK IS ALL ABOUT!

We believe this unique cookbook will become your favorite cookbook. We are excited to share this astonishing collection of recipes inspired by truly incredible restaurants. We hope you will *LOVE* them as much as we do!

Bon Appétit! Chef Bob and Chef Ellen

P.S. *Special Bonus…*if you are vacationing in beautiful Oregon, we have 2 *not-to-be-missed* restaurant recommendations for you. In our Main Event chapter, read about Restaurant Beck and Marché Restaurant with an exceptional recipe from each of these extraordinary restaurants.

To Begin…

Appetizers, Small Plates, and Cocktail Hour Nibbles

The Ceviche Martini with Avocado and Ginger 11

Bruschetta with Tomatoes, Basil and Garlic 13

Love Boats! 15

Smoked Salmon Pâté with Fresh Dill 17

Pan Sautéed Fresh Mushrooms with Garlic and Vermouth 19

Eggplant Crostini with Smoked Paprika and Fresh Oregano 20

Sinful Scampi, Pan Sautéed 21

Shrimp on the Barbie with Fresh Lime 21

Chunky Guacamole with Fresh Tomatoes and Jalapeños 22

Hummus on Naan Bread 23

The Ceviche Martini with Avocado and Ginger

What a wonderful way to start a dinner party!
An exquisite presentation…. and it tastes even better than it looks!
Since the fish cooks in fresh lime juice, be sure all the seafood is *very* fresh. A specialty
fish market will provide you with the freshest and the best quality.

The Ceviche Martini with Avocado and Ginger

1 cup freshly squeezed lime juice, approximately 6 limes required
½ sweet onion, chopped
2 large shrimp, shelled and deveined
2 ounces fresh cod
2 ounces wild fresh salmon
1 large diver scallop or 4 small scallops
1 tomato, cut up in ½ inch cubes
¼ cup fresh dill, freshly chopped
½ cup fresh cilantro leaves only
1 ripe avocado, diced and cubed
1 fresh jalapeño, deseeded, minced
2 tablespoons fresh ginger, sliced and finely minced

Marinate fish & shellfish for 4 hours in lime juice and onion.
Drain off liquid.
Add tomato, cilantro, avocado, jalapeño, dill and ginger to fish.
Refrigerate 4 hours before serving.
Show off the colors by serving in a large martini glass.
Serves 4
Approximately 181 calories per serving.

Bruschetta with Tomatoes, Basil and Garlic

Open a chilled bottle of Pinot Gris and step out on your deck with your friends as the sun sets in the west. Savor a delicious bruschetta, sip the wine, and watch the sun disappear on the horizon. Life is good!

Bruschetta with Tomatoes, Basil and Garlic

2 rounds of naan bread, sliced into 6 triangles each
2 medium vine ripened tomatoes, coarsely chopped and juice drained
½ cup fresh basil leaves, chopped
3 cloves of garlic, minced
1 tablespoon quality extra virgin olive oil

Heat naan bread triangles on a baking sheet in the oven at 400 degrees for 3 minutes.
Mix tomatoes, garlic and basil with olive oil and pile high onto naan bread.
Serves 4 (3 triangles per person)
Approximately 204 calories per serving.

TIPS FROM THE CHEFS: *We love toppings served on naan bread, but it can also be served on a soft no pocket pita or on crusty French bread crostini.*

Love Boats!

If you are a raving fan of chicken lettuce wraps… you'll love these!

Love Boats!

To prepare ingredients for the filling, pulse for 2 seconds in your food processor until coarsely chopped but not puréed:

2 chicken breasts, skinless, boneless

Sliced water chestnuts, 6 ounces

2 cloves of garlic

1 tablespoon fresh ginger, chopped

1 jalapeño, seeds and ribs removed, cut into small pieces

8 crimini mushrooms, washed and stems removed

3 green onions, cleaned and outer skin removed

To prepare cooking sauce, whisk these ingredients together:

3 tablespoons sesame oil

1 tablespoon chili oil

1 tablespoon sweet chili sauce

1 tablespoon fresh ginger, minced

1 teaspoon Chinese Five Spice seasoning

3 cloves fresh garlic, crushed

1 tablespoon light soy sauce

1 tablespoon brown sugar

2 tablespoons toasted sesame seeds

4 heads of Belgian endive:

Wash and peel leaves off separately. Store cups in paper towels in the refrigerator to dry and crisp.

2 ounces uncooked Chinese bean threads: Heat vegetable oil over high heat. Test temperature by putting 1 thread in the hot oil. Oil is ready when test thread immediately puffs up. Flash fry small amounts of bean threads in vegetable oil for 15 seconds until they "explode." Repeat until you have the desired quantity. Place each batch on paper towels to drain excess oil.

Stir fry filling ingredients in cooking sauce for 5-7 minutes.

Serve over a bed of crispy bean threads in a family style serving dish.

Serve with a separate plate of chilled Belgian endive leaves.

People take a leaf, spoon in the chicken filling and season it with their choice of sauces: Chinese mustard, chili paste, hoisin or plum sauce.

Serves 4

Approximately 310 calories per serving.

Smoked Salmon Pâté with Fresh Dill

Of all the recipes for appetizers, this is one of the simplest, most delicious, and easiest to make! The key is to use the best quality smoked salmon you can find. Smoke the salmon yourself or buy from a specialty seafood store that smokes their own salmon.

Smoked Salmon Pâté with Fresh Dill

10 ounces smoked salmon
8   ounces low fat cream cheese
2   tablespoons freshly squeezed lemon juice
6   tablespoons fresh dill, chopped (reserve 3 tablespoons for garnish)
3   tablespoons fresh chives, chopped

Mix all ingredients (including 3 tablespoons of the dill) together in a food processor and pulse for 8 to10 seconds.

Put pâté in a small porcelain serving dish. Cover with plastic wrap and refrigerate for 3 hours or more.

Remove from the refrigerator and garnish with the reserved 3 tablespoons of chopped fresh dill. Serve on small plates with your favorite crackers.

Serves 4

Approximately 220 calories per serving

Pan Sautéed Fresh Mushrooms with Garlic and Vermouth

This recipe was inspired by a great French bistro in Paris. You have never tasted mushrooms this delicious…and healthy too!

Pan Sautéed Fresh Mushrooms with Garlic and Vermouth

12 ounces fresh mushrooms (shiitake and crimini are great…or a mixture of any 2 or 3 fresh mushrooms)
2   tablespoons unsalted butter
1   cup dry vermouth
3   cloves garlic, minced
1   tablespoon fresh lemon juice
Fresh ground pepper
½   cup fresh minced dill (save for garnish)

Wash and clean mushrooms, cut into bite sized pieces and place in mixing bowl.
Sauté garlic in butter for 2-3 minutes.
Sauté mushrooms at medium high heat for 2 minutes in butter and garlic.
Add ½ cup vermouth and lemon juice. Pan sauté on high heat for 1-2 additional minutes.
Transfer mushrooms to serving plates.
Add ½ cup vermouth and 1 tablespoon butter to make additional sauce.
Serve on heated plates. Pour sauce over mushrooms.
Garnish with dill.
Serve with sour dough bread to soak up sauce.
Serves 4
Approximately 123 calories per serving (calories for bread not included).

TIPS FROM THE CHEFS: *Did you know that mushrooms are the only vegetable with natural vitamin D? (report from mushroomcouncil.com)*

A great way to start the evening! Incredibly delicious…easy to prepare.

Eggplant Crostini with Smoked Paprika and Fresh Oregano

1 large eggplant
2 small tomatoes, quartered
1 tablespoon extra virgin olive oil
1 sweet onion, quartered
1 clove garlic, quartered
2 red peppers, blackened (see instructions below)
1 jalapeño, seeded, deveined, and minced

½ teaspoon smoked paprika
½ teaspoon regular paprika
4 sprigs fresh oregano, leaves removed
4 tablespoons freshly squeezed lemon juice
Freshly ground pepper
2 naan breads, cut into quarters (reserve for serving)
1 tablespoon unsalted butter, melted (reserve for naan bread)

Place whole red peppers under broiler to blacken skin. Cool. Put in plastic bag (15 minutes). Cut peppers open, rinse, remove seeds, and charred skin.

Boil whole eggplant, skin on, at medium for 1 hour. Cool and remove skin.

Put top 12 ingredients in food processor. Pulse until coarsely chopped (about 5 seconds). Put in serving bowl and chill for 2 hours.

Brush both sides of naan bread slices with melted butter and bake for 3 minutes at 400 degrees. Top naan breads with eggplant mixture.

(You can substitute sour dough baguette slices for naan bread, as shown)

Serves 4

Approximately 228 calories per serving.

Eggplant Crostini with Smoked Paprika and Fresh Oregano

Try our two all-time favorite shrimp recipes…one now…one another time. You'll love them both!

Just a little bit bad, but oh…so good!

Sinful Scampi

12 large wild caught shrimp (12-15 to a pound), shelled, cleaned, and deveined
1 cup bread crumbs

2 tablespoons extra virgin olive oil
2 cloves garlic, minced
Parsley, freshly chopped for garnish

Dip shrimp in a little olive oil. Roll each shrimp in bread crumbs until covered on all sides.
Pan sauté shrimp at medium high heat in remaining olive oil and garlic, turning once. Shrimp will turn pink when done.
Serve on heated plates. Garnish with chopped parsley.
Serves 4 (3 shrimp per serving as a first course)
Approximately 258 calories per serving.

Shrimp on the Barbie…perfect with a chilled glass of
New Zealand Sauvignon Blanc!

Shrimp on the Barbie with Fresh Lime

12 large wild caught shrimp, (12-15 to a pound), shelled, cleaned, and deveined
½ cup fresh cilantro, chopped (reserve ¼ cup for garnish)

3 garlic cloves, finely minced
Juice of 2 fresh limes
1 teaspoon red pepper flakes
4 tablespoons unsalted butter, melted

Marinate the shrimp in cilantro, garlic, lime juice and red pepper flakes for 30 minutes. Just before grilling toss in melted butter.
Grill shrimp in a wire basket directly over the flame on the barbeque for 2 to 3 minutes per side until pink. Shrimp may get a little charred…that is good!
Serve immediately on heated plates. Garnish with chopped cilantro.
Serves 4 (3 shrimp per serving as a first course)
Approximately 196 calories per serving.

**A big bowl of Chunky Guacamole, some crisp corn tortilla chips,
and a bottle of ice cold Dos Equis...life is good!**

Chunky Guacamole with Fresh Tomatoes and Jalapeños

2 ripe avocados
2 tablespoons fresh lime juice
½ sweet onion, finely chopped
4 drops Tabasco
1 garlic clove, minced
1 jalapeño, deseeded, finely minced
1 small tomato, diced, juice discarded
2 tablespoons fresh cilantro, chopped

Cut avocados in half. Remove seeds. Scoop out avocado and dice into ¼ inch chunks. Toss avocado with fresh lime juice, Tabasco, garlic, onions and jalapeño. Add tomato and cilantro and toss gently.
Chill for 4 hours, covered, in the refrigerator.
Serves 4
Approximately 190 calories per serving not including chips and beer!

Chunky Guacamole with Fresh Tomatoes
and Jalapeños

Hummus on Naan Bread

2   rounds of naan bread, sliced into 6 triangles each
1   15.5 ounce can low sodium garbanzo beans
5   tablespoons tahini
2   tablespoons olive oil
3   garlic cloves, minced
Juice of 1 lemon (1/4 cup)
½   teaspoon cayenne
½   teaspoon cumin
Pinch of salt
Freshly ground pepper
Paprika to dust top

Blend garbanzo beans, olive oil and tahini in food processor.
Add garlic, lemon juice, cayenne, cumin, salt and pepper.
Chill hummus 1-2 hours.
Heat naan bread on baking sheet in oven at 400 degrees for 3 minutes.
Pile hummus on bread and sprinkle with paprika.
Serves 4 (3 triangles per person)
Approximately 455 calories per 3 triangle
serving.

Hummus on Naan Bread

Sensational Salads

Shrimp Salad with Mango, Avocado and Red Pepper 27

Crab Louie, King of Salads 29

Salad Nicoise with Wild Caught Albacore Tuna 31

Beet Salad with Goat Cheese, House Roasted Pecans 33

Imperial Palace Chinese Chicken Salad 35

Chopped Italian Salad with Avocado, Red Pepper, Feta 37

Classic Caesar Salad with House Made Garlic Croutons 39

Watercress and Crumbled Feta Cheese Salad 41

Mango, Frisee and Watercress Chicken Salad 42

Southwestern Chicken Salad 43

Greek Salad with Kalamata Olives and Feta Cheese 44

Summer Salad with Red Pepper, Avocado and Peaches 45

Bistro Potato Salad with Fresh Dill 46

Santa Fe Grilled Shrimp and Corn Salad 47

Arugula, Mint and Goat Cheese Salad 49

Shrimp Salad with Mango, Avocado, and Red Pepper

**This incredibly flavorful salad makes a great main course.
Your family and guests will love it!**

Shrimp Salad with Mango, Avocado, and Red Pepper

16 large shrimp (12-15 count), remove shells and devein
1   head arugula, wash, spin dry and chill
½ cup garbanzo beans
1   mango, cut up in slices
½ red onion, sliced and chopped
1   red pepper, sliced and chopped
1   avocado, cut up in slices
    Freshly ground black pepper

Dressing:
3   tablespoons olive oil
3   tablespoons lemon juice
2   cloves of garlic, minced
2   tablespoons fresh dill, finely chopped

Bring 2 cups of water to a boil, put shrimp in the boiling water and turn the temperature down to simmer. Cook 3 minutes until shrimp turn pink.
Remove shrimp and place in cold water bath to chill.

To make dressing, whisk lemon juice into oil, 1 drop at a time. Add dill and garlic.
To make salad, combine all ingredients except shrimp and toss with dressing. Place salad on chilled salad plates and put 4 large shrimp on each salad.
Serves 4
Approximately 378 calories per serving.

Crab Louie, King of Salads

The king of salads, the one and only Crab Louie, unbeatable when made
with fresh Dungeness crab and our special Louie Dressing!

Crab Louie, King of Salads

1   pound Dungeness crab*, picked over, including a generous amount of crab legs
2   eggs, hard boiled
1   head romaine lettuce
24 Nicoise black olives, seed in
8   green onions, peeled, washed, and sliced into 1" pieces
24 ripe cherry tomatoes
2   tablespoons fresh chopped dill

Louie Dressing:
½ cup light mayonnaise
¼ cup chili sauce
¼ cup light sour cream
¼ teaspoon cayenne pepper
2   tablespoons fresh lemon juice

Toss chilled fresh romaine in 4 tablespoons of Louie Dressing.
Then compose all other salad ingredients and place over the bed of romaine. Divide salad onto
4 chilled dinner plates. Top it with a drizzle of Louie dressing over each serving. Add freshly
cracked pepper and garnish with fresh dill. Serve with lemon wedges.
Serves 4
Approximately 355 calories per serving.
*Special Note: If Dungeness crab is not available where you live you can use any fresh crab meat
that is available. You can also substitute bay shrimp for crab and enjoy a Shrimp Louie…equally
delicious and about the same in calories!

TIPS FROM THE CHEFS: *Olives (technically fruits) are bursting with disease blocking antioxidants, monosaturated (good)*
fats, iron and vitamin E! Buy them whole, not pitted or stuffed, for biggest health advantage. Black olives contain more cancer
preventing flavonoids than green olives. (realage.com)

Salad Nicoise with Wild Caught Albacore Tuna

Salad Nicoise...a work of art on a plate!
Your family and guests will love this healthy one dish dinner.

Salad Nicoise with Wild Caught Albacore Tuna

4   hard boiled eggs (13 minutes in gently boiling water, chill, cut in half)
16 cherry tomatoes
7   ounce can of premium quality wild albacore tuna, drained and chilled
20 Nicoise olives, seed in (or substitute Kalamata olives)
8   green onions, peeled, washed, trimmed, served whole

1   pound green beans, trimmed (3 minutes in gently boiling water, then plunge into cold water to stop cooking and chill)
Fresh dill (for garnish)
4   Yukon Gold potatoes
Capers (for garnish)

Dressing:
2   tablespoons extra virgin olive oil
8   tablespoons lemon juice freshly squeezed (2 lemons)
2   teaspoons Dijon mustard
3   green onions, chopped

2   shallots, minced
2   cloves of garlic, minced
4   tablespoons fresh chopped dill
Fresh ground pepper to taste

Make potato salad:
Cut potatoes into ½ inch cubes and boil for 5 minutes (test after 4 minutes). Plunge into cold water to stop cooking. Drain.
Toss potatoes with 6 tablespoons of dressing and chill.

Chill all ingredients until serving.
To serve, compose all ingredients on large chilled plates, using color and texture to create a beautiful plate. Drizzle the rest of the dressing over all. Garnish with capers and chopped fresh dill.
Serves 4
Approximately 375 calories per serving.
Black beans, marinated in dressing, can replace potato salad.
See photo at beginning of this chapter.

Beet Salad with Goat Cheese and House Roasted Pecans

Beets are beautiful! This often overlooked vegetable is nutritious and absolutely stunning on the plate. Try this salad as a first course and then add a delicious soup for a superb summer dinner.

Beet Salad with Goat Cheese and House Roasted Pecans

6   red beets, equal in size
1   cup baby greens
1   tablespoon extra virgin olive oil
2   tablespoons sherry
2   tablespoons rice wine vinegar
Thyme, fresh leaves removed from 4 stems
Fresh ground pepper
½   cup house roasted raw pecan halves (27 minutes at 325 degrees)
4   ounces goat cheese, coarsely crumbled

Do not peel beets. Wash them gently and leave 1 inch of the stems and tail on. Put them into boiling hot water and then reduce heat to medium for 35 minutes. Test. When tender, remove the beets from the hot liquid and plunge into cold water. Now it's easy to remove skin. Cool and slice beets into ¼ inch rounds.

Whisk together the sherry, rice vinegar, olive oil, thyme and pepper. Add the beet slices and marinate in the refrigerator for several hours, stirring occasionally. Remove beets and use marinade to dress greens.
Add pecans. Arrange greens on chilled salad plates and top with a row of beet rounds. Sprinkle with crumbled goat cheese.
Serves 4
Approximately 178 calories per serving.

Imperial Palace Chicken Salad

This recipe is our version of the famous Chinese Chicken Salad from the legendary Imperial Palace Restaurant in San Francisco. Sadly, the original Imperial Palace has closed. This is the finest Chinese chicken salad we have ever experienced.

Imperial Palace Chinese Chicken Salad

8-10 ounces poached chicken breast, julienned lengthwise (2 ½ inches long)
1   small (3/4) head crisp romaine lettuce, outside leaves removed, shredded
½ cucumber, finely julienned 2 ½ inches long
1   carrot, finely julienned 2 ½ inches long
1   bunch scallions (green onions sliced lengthwise, 2 ½ inches long)
2   tablespoons fresh ginger root, chopped very finely
3   tablespoons roasted peanuts
1   cup fresh cilantro sprigs (2/3 cup in salad, reserve 1/3 cup for garnish)

The dressing is the secret!
3   tablespoons sesame oil
3   tablespoons rice wine vinegar
1   tablespoon low sodium soy sauce
1   tablespoon hot pepper oil (Asian)
2   tablespoons sesame seeds, toasted
1   tablespoon Chinese five spice seasoning
1   tablespoon sweet chili sauce
1   tablespoon brown sugar
1   tablespoon finely chopped fresh ginger

2 ounces uncooked Chinese bean threads: Heat vegetable oil over high heat. Test temperature by putting 1 thread in the hot oil. Oil is ready when test thread immediately puffs up. Flash fry small amounts of bean threads in vegetable oil for 15 seconds until they "explode." Repeat until you have the desired quantity. Place each batch on paper towels to drain excess oil.

Combine the salad ingredients. Add the dressing and toss.
Top with the crispy bean threads just before serving. Garnish with cilantro.
Serves 2 for entrée salad and 4 as a first course salad
Approximately 390 calories per serving.

Chopped Italian Salad with Avocado, Red Pepper and Feta

This is one of Chef Ellen's favorite luncheon salads, discovered in an Italian restaurant in Los Angeles years ago. It lingers in memory and begs to be revisited!

Chopped Italian Salad with Avocado, Red Pepper and Feta

8 leaves crisp romaine, chopped
⅓ green cabbage, chopped
2 chicken breasts, boneless, skinless, poached and sliced
1 cucumber, peeled and chopped
1 red bell pepper, chopped
½ red onion, chopped
1 avocado, cut into ½ inch cubes
3 slices bacon, fried crispy, broken up
2 tablespoons fresh oregano leaves
6 large fresh basil leaves, chopped
1 15.5 oz can low sodium garbanzo beans
4 ounces feta cheese, crumbled

Dressing:
1 clove of garlic, minced
1 shallot, finely chopped
2 teaspoons Dijon mustard
3 tablespoons wine vinegar
2 tablespoons lemon juice
2 tablespoons extra virgin olive oil (see product page)
  Cracked black pepper

Chop all salad ingredients about the same size. Combine with dressing.
Serve each salad on 2 romaine leaves and garnish with crumbled feta.
Serves 4
Approximately 452 calories per serving.

Classic Caesar Salad with House Made Garlic Croutons

**Many say this is the best Caesar salad they ever tasted. A made from scratch
Caesar is such a treat! Try this version and you'll never settle for less.**

Classic Caesar Salad with House Made Garlic Croutons

1 head romaine
2 pieces flat anchovies
4 ounces imported Reggiano Parmigiano cheese, freshly grated
1 coddled egg, well beaten (coddle in boiling water 60 seconds)
4 tablespoons extra virgin olive oil (reserve 2 tablespoons for croutons)

5 cloves garlic, crushed (reserve 3 cloves for croutons)
3 tablespoons freshly squeezed lemon juice
1 tablespoon Worcestershire sauce
5 dashes Tabasco
Freshly ground black pepper
3 thick (½ inch) slices of sourdough bread

To make croutons:
Cut bread into ¾ inch wide cubes. Toss croutons in olive oil and garlic.
Spread on a baking sheet so they are not touching each other.
Bake at 350 degrees for 20 minutes, tossing halfway through.
Make croutons early in the day and store until ready to mix into salad.

To make salad:
Remove outer leaves from romaine, twist off top of head, wash well, and dry well. Chill in refrigerator in paper towels until crisp and cold.
Cut anchovies into small pieces, place in a large salad bowl with olive oil and crushed garlic.
Crush anchovies with a fork to blend together.
Tear romaine leaves into bite size pieces and put in a salad bowl with oil and garlic. Add beaten coddled egg and toss with greens.
Add lemon juice, Tabasco, and Worcestershire. Toss with greens.
Add fresh ground pepper and croutons and toss with greens.
Top with grated Reggiano Parmigiano cheese and freshly ground pepper.
Serve immediately on chilled salad plates with chilled salad forks.
Serves 4
Approximately 340 calories per serving.

Watercress and Crumbled Feta Cheese Salad

A fresh watercress salad is a beautiful beginning to a chilled salad and soup dinner. For a perfect summer day, prepare both when it's cool in the morning and serve easily in the evening!

Watercress and Crumbled Feta Cheese Salad

2 heads watercress, stems removed
3 green onions, sliced into 1 inch pieces
1 cup garbanzo beans
Freshly ground black pepper
4 ounces of crumbled feta cheese

Whisk together for dressing:
3 tablespoons walnut oil (see product page)
3 tablespoons lemon juice

Combine watercress, onions, and garbanzos in salad bowl.
Cover with plastic wrap, and chill.
Toss with dressing just prior to serving and serve on chilled plates.
Grind pepper over each salad and top with crumbled feta cheese.
Serves 4
Approximately 250 calories per serving.

**An extraordinary salad! Frisee is a bitter green, light, airy and delicious. Watercress
balances beautifully with its peppery flavor. Mango sends it to the moon!**

Mango, Frisee and Watercress Chicken Salad

2   chicken breasts, boneless, skinless
1   head of frisee, washed, dried, and chilled
1   head of watercress, leaves removed
    from stems, washed, dried, and chilled
1   vine ripened tomato, sliced and diced
½   red pepper, sliced and diced
1   mango, peeled and cubed

½   cup low sodium garbanzo beans
¼   red onion, sliced and diced
4   ounces blue cheese, crumbled
    (reserve for garnish)
¼   cup fresh dill, finely chopped
2   teaspoons curry powder
Fresh ground black pepper

Dressing:
2   tablespoons fresh lemon juice
2   tablespoons extra virgin olive oil
1   garlic clove, finely minced

Rub curry powder into the chicken breasts. Grill chicken in a fry pan over medium heat, turning
once until cooked through, 13 minutes total.
Allow chicken to rest 3 minutes. Slice
chicken into ¼ inch strips.
Combine all salad ingredients, dress salad
and top with chicken.
Add fresh ground pepper. Serve on chilled
salad plates.
Serves 4
Approximately 352 calories per serving.

Mango, Frisee and Watercress Chicken Salad

We discovered this spectacular salad in Arizona. The southwestern flavors and colors of this stunning salad are wonderful, especially complemented by the delicious Cilantro Lime Vinaigrette!

Southwestern Chicken Salad

1   head of romaine, outside leaves discarded, washed, chilled and broken into bite size pieces
1   chicken breast (6-8 ounces, boneless and skinless)
½   cup jicama slices
½   cup, dried cranberries, sliced
½   cup pecans, roasted
2   cobs of corn
4   ounces Swiss cheese, julienned
½   red pepper, sliced
½   avocado, sliced
¼   red onion, finely sliced
½   cup fresh mint leaves

Cilantro Lime Vinaigrette:
Fresh lime juice of three limes
2   garlic cloves, crushed
1   cup cilantro, chopped
3   tablespoons apple cider vinegar
¼   teaspoon cayenne
1   teaspoon cumin
3   tablespoons extra virgin olive oil

Whisk together all ingredients for the vinaigrette.
Roast the corn over flame on the grill (about 8 minutes) and slice off corn kernels. Chill.
Poach or grill the chicken, cut into cubes and chill.
Combine all the salad ingredients .
Dress the salad and serve on chilled plates.
Serves 4
Approximately 589 calories per serving.

For a delightful summer supper, start with a bowl of chilled soup and
then enjoy this "Big Fat" Greek Salad as a main course!

Greek Salad with Kalamata Olives and Feta Cheese

½ red onion, cut in ½ inch chunks
½ sweet onion, cut in ½ inch chunks
2   red peppers, cut in ½ inch cubes
2   cucumbers, peeled and cut into ½ inch cubes
8   cherry tomatoes, cut in half
16 Kalamata olives, with pits, rinsed
Leaves from 6 fresh oregano stems
4   ounces crumbled feta cheese (reserve for topping)

Greek Salad Dressing:
4   tablespoons olive oil
6   garlic cloves, finely chopped
8   tablespoons lemon juice
½ teaspoon sugar
Fresh ground black pepper

Combine all salad ingredients
above (except cheese) and toss
with salad dressing. Top with
crumbled feta cheese. Serve on
chilled dinner plates.
Serves 4
Approximately 323 calories per
serving.

Greek Salad with Kalamata Olives
and Feta Cheese

Sunshine, soft breezes, patio dining, peaches, avocado, mint…we love the fresh smells and tastes of summer!

Summer Salad with Red Pepper, Avocado and Peaches

2   chicken breasts, 7 ounces each, boneless and skinless, poached and sliced into bite size
    sections
1   head of romaine lettuce, outside leaves removed, top twisted off and leaves broken up into
    bite size pieces
¼   cup fresh whole mint leaves
6   green onions, sliced ¼ inch
½   cup jicama, julienned
½   cup gruyere cheese, julienned
1   ripe summer peach, peeled, seeded, and sliced ½ inch
½   cup sliced almonds, pan toasted in 1 teaspoon of butter
½   red pepper, cut into ½ inch cubes
1   avocado, cubed
Freshly ground black pepper

Dressing:
2   tablespoons walnut oil
2   tablespoons rice wine vinegar

Toss salad ingredients with dressing and serve on chilled plates.
Serves 4
Approximately 465 calories per serving.

Bistro Potato Salad with Fresh Dill

5   medium size Yukon Gold potatoes
8   green onions

Dressing:
¼   cup light mayonnaise
¼   cup rice wine vinegar
¼   cup Dijon mustard
2   teaspoons caraway seeds
1   large bunch fresh dill, washed, dried and finely minced (remove stems before chopping)

Wash and peel potatoes. Cut them into ½ inch cubes. Cook 5 minutes in gently boiling water (Test at 4 minutes. Do not allow potatoes to get overcooked). Wash and peel green onions. Remove beards and cut off green tops. Slice into ¼ inch pieces.
Whisk dressing until smooth, toss with green onions, caraway seeds, half of the dill and cubed potatoes.
Chill 1 hour or more.
Garnish with other half of fresh dill and freshly cracked pepper.
Serves 4
Approximately 185 calories per serving.

Bistro Potato Salad with Fresh Dill

Southwestern cuisine is a blend of Native American, Hispanic and Anglo culinary traditions. These dishes can make you cry from the heat or beg for more with the amazing flavors of chile peppers, corn, and native herbs and spices. Here is a recipe inspired by one of our favorite Santa Fe restaurants!

Santa Fe Grilled Shrimp and Corn Salad

16 large shrimp, (12-15 to a pound) peeled and deveined
2   cups romaine lettuce, washed, dried, broken up into bite size pieces
4   ears of fresh corn
1   tablespoon olive oil to coat corn and shrimp
1   cup black beans
1   jalapeño, minced finely
1   red onion, chopped finely
½   cup loosely packed fresh cilantro leaves, chopped finely
4   ounces goat cheese, crumbled

Dressing:
4   tablespoons fresh lemon juice
3   tablespoons extra virgin olive oil (in addition to oil for coating corn and shrimp)
1   teaspoon freshly ground black pepper

Brush the corn with oil and grill it directly on the hot grate, turning until the kernels are golden brown all over, about 8 minutes total. Cut the kernels from the cobs and reserve.
Brush the shrimp with oil. Grill 2 minutes on each side over a wire grid.
Mix together the greens, onion, jalapeño, shrimp, corn, black beans, and cilantro.
For the dressing, whisk together the lemon juice and oil. Combine all ingredients and pour the dressing over the salad, sprinkle with black pepper, and toss.
Serve on chilled dinner plates. Top with crumbled goat cheese.
Serves 4
Approximately 322 calories per serving. (Incredible with homemade
corn bread but add 100 calories!)

Arugula, Mint, and Goat Cheese Salad

You'll love this unique combination of flavors to begin a memorable dinner!

Arugula, Mint, and Goat Cheese Salad

Arugula, greens for 4, washed and dried
10 large fresh mint leaves
2   ounces goat cheese, in chunks
½   cup garbanzo beans
3   ounces toasted pine nuts

Dressing:
2   tablespoons fresh lemon juice
2   tablespoons quality extra virgin olive oil

Whisk together oil and lemon juice. Combine salad ingredients and toss dressing with salad.
Serve on chilled salad plates.
Serves 4
Approximately 192 calories per serving.

TIPS FROM THE CHEFS: *Another way to serve this salad is to substitute imported Reggiano Parmigiano cheese, freshly grated over the greens, for the goat cheese. This is an entirely different orchestration and equally delicious!*

Super Soups

Our All Time Favorite Clam Chowder

Our guests say this is the best clam chowder they've ever tasted!
We tested dozens of clam chowders in Maine and Oregon before we developed this recipe.
Now it's your turn to see what you think. It's the secret missing ingredient that makes this
chowder so yummy! It's made <u>without flour</u> resulting in an incredibly delicious broth!

Our All Time Favorite Clam Chowder

16 fresh manila clams in shells
8   ounces chopped cooked clams available at your fish market
12 ounces low sodium chicken broth
3   medium Yukon Gold potatoes, peeled and cut into ½ inch cubes
1   sweet onion, chopped
2   teaspoons unsalted butter
1   cup half and half cream
4   dashes Tabasco
1   tablespoon Worcestershire sauce
½ cup fresh dill, chopped
Fresh ground pepper to taste

Sauté chopped onion in butter.
Cook potato cubes in chicken stock until fork tender, about 5 minutes.
Add onions to cooked potato and broth.
Add Tabasco and Worcestershire. Bring to a boil. Reduce temperature to medium-high.
Add fresh clams in shells. Cook until shells open (3-5 minutes).
Add chopped clams and heat for 3 minutes on low heat.
Heat half and half in a separate pot until steaming hot but do not boil.
Pour chowder into bowls and top off with the heated half and half.
Garnish with chopped fresh dill.
Serve piping hot in heated soup bowls.
Serves 4
Approximately 200 calories per serving.

Gazpacho with Bay Shrimp

Gazpacho is the quintessential chilled soup, absolutely delicious when served with a fresh green salad. It becomes a perfect Sunday night supper. It's garlicky, spicy, healthy, delicious, and filling. All this and low calorie too!

Gazpacho with Bay Shrimp

3   cups chopped tomatoes (see Product page)
2   tablespoons rice wine vinegar
1   large cucumber, peeled and cut into chunks
2   red bell peppers
3   large garlic cloves, crushed
1   tablespoon olive oil
2   teaspoons cumin
¼   teaspoon cayenne
4   dashes of Tabasco sauce
4   tablespoons chopped fresh dill (reserve 2 tablespoons dill for garnish)
8   ounces of fresh cooked bay shrimp (reserve for topping gazpacho)

Combine all ingredients in food processor with the exception of the bay shrimp and dill. Pulse ingredients until coarsely chopped.
Chill 8 hours in refrigerator.
To serve, put 1 cup in each chilled soup plate.
Top each serving with 4 ounces of bay shrimp and garnish with freshly chopped dill.
Serves 4
Approximately 150 calories per serving.

Hot and Sour Chinese Soup

Bursts of Asian flavors spark this spicy Chinese soup! Low in calories yet high in nutrition, it will soon become your family favorite!

Hot and Sour Chinese Soup

1 chicken breast (about 7 ounces) boneless and skinless, cut into ½ inch cubes
4 cups low sodium chicken broth (see Product page)
2 tablespoons rice vinegar
1 tablespoon low sodium soy sauce
1 teaspoon sesame oil
1½ tablespoons hot chili oil
1 teaspoon freshly ground pepper
6 ounces water chestnuts, sliced
8 fresh shiitake mushrooms, stems removed and sliced in ¼ inch pieces
1 cup sherry
1 egg, beaten
4 ounces fresh snow peas
4 ounces tofu, cut into small cubes
½ cup farfalle (dried pasta)
3 green onions, thinly sliced (reserved for garnish)

Stir together rice vinegar, soy sauce, sesame oil, chili oil and pepper and reserve.
Bring the chicken broth to boil over medium high heat in a soup pot.
Add chicken, mushrooms, pasta, and water chestnuts and cook 8 minutes.
Add the reserved oil and vinegar mixture and sherry. Reduce the heat to lowest setting.
Slowly add the beaten egg in droplets.
Turn heat up to high and add snow peas and tofu and cook for 2 minutes.
Serve steaming hot in heated bowls.
Garnish with sliced green onions.
Serves 4
Approximately 233 calories per serving.

Chicken Soup Like Grandma Used to Make…but Better!

Perfect for those nights when you just want a bowl of delicious hot soup for supper.
It will cure whatever ails you. So good you could eat it right out of the pot!

Chicken Soup Like Grandma Used to Make...but Better!

1   large sweet onion peeled and chopped
1   tablespoon extra virgin olive oil
2   chicken breasts (about 7 ounces each), boneless and skinless, cubed
32 ounces low-sodium chicken broth (see product page)
2   cups dry vermouth
3   cloves garlic, chopped
3   carrots, peeled and ¼ inch sliced
2   parsnips, peeled and ¼ inch sliced
1   turnip, peeled and 1 inch cubed
2   medium Yukon Gold potatoes, peeled and 1 inch cubed
8   crimini mushrooms, ½ inch sliced
1   sweet red pepper, diced
¼   teaspoon cayenne
½   teaspoon cumin
½   teaspoon curry powder
Thyme, fresh (put in several whole sprigs, remove twigs before serving)
or ½ teaspoon dried
1   bay leaf
6   whole cloves
Lots of cracked black pepper

Caramelize onion in olive oil for 20 minutes at medium high heat in a large soup pot, stirring frequently. Add all other ingredients. Cover, bring to a boil, reduce heat to simmer. Cook for 1 hour.
Serve in heated large soup plates.
Serves 4
Approximately 379 calories per serving.

Mama Mia Minestrone

It's so much fun to go to the farmers markets for vegetables freshly picked that very morning...and even more fun to bring them home to make this extraordinary minestrone. It's vegetable soup-just like Mama used to make!

Mama Mia Minestrone!

1   sweet onion, peeled and chopped
2   tablespoons olive oil
4   cups low sodium chicken broth (see product page)
1   carrot, peeled and diced
1   celery stalk, diced
1   zucchini, diced
1   yellow summer squash, diced
1   Yukon Gold potato, peeled and cubed
2   large fresh tomatoes, sliced and cubed
1   cup fresh green beans, ends removed, cut into 1 inch sections
3   large garlic cloves, finely chopped
½   cup chopped tomatoes
1   cup cannellini beans, cooked
½   cup fresh basil, chopped
½   cup fresh oregano, chopped
1   teaspoon red pepper flakes
Fresh ground black pepper
4   tablespoons Parmigiano Reggiano cheese, grated (for garnish)

Caramelize onion in 2 tablespoons olive oil at medium high in a large soup pan for 20 minutes. Stir frequently.
Add chicken broth and then other ingredients except green beans.
Cover, bring to a boil, and immediately reduce to simmer 1 hour.
Add green beans 3 minutes before serving.
Serve very hot in heated soup plates.
Garnish with freshly grated Parmigiano Reggiano cheese.
Serves 4
Approximately 300 calories per serving.

Chilled Beet Borscht with Sour Cream and Green Onions

We were introduced to this exceptional soup years ago at the Russian Tea Room in New York. Our version, adapted to today's palate, is a wonderful soup served ice cold on a hot summer day!

Chilled Beet Borscht with Sour Cream and Green Onions

6 red beets, peeled
Juice from 2 lemons
4 cups water
2 tablespoons sugar
Pinch salt
6 cloves
8 tablespoons sour cream (reserve for garnish)
4 green onions, diced (reserve for garnish)

Do not peel beets. Wash them gently and leave 1 inch of the stems and tail on. Put them into boiling hot water and then reduce heat to medium for 35 minutes. Test. When tender, remove the beets from the hot liquid and plunge into cold water. Now it's easy to remove skin. Cool and grate the beets.

Add lemon juice, sugar, pinch of salt, cloves and 4 cups of fresh water to grated beets and simmer for 15 minutes.

Cool, cover and refrigerate 4-6 hours before serving.

Garnish with a dollop of sour cream and diced green onions just before serving. Serve in chilled soup bowls.

Serves 4

Approximately 79 calories per serving.

TIPS FROM THE CHEFS: *Another way to present this soup is to whisk the sour cream into the soup before serving. This changes the color to a beautiful light red and gives it a different spin.*

**You just started your new weight loss plan. No problem! This hearty, healthy
and deeply flavorful vegetarian chili is the perfect answer!**

Cold Day! Hot Chili!

2 tablespoons extra virgin olive oil
3 large sweet onions, chopped
4 garlic cloves, chopped
1 tablespoon ground cumin
1 teaspoon dried oregano
4 tablespoons chili powder
1 tablespoon paprika
½ cup dry sherry

3 cups chopped tomatoes (see product page)
1 cup tomato juice
1 yellow pepper, sliced, and chopped
1 jalapeño, seeds removed and chopped
¾ cup dried black beans, cooked
¾ cup dried red kidney beans, cooked
4 tablespoons low fat sour cream
    (see product page) (for topping)
2 green onions, thinly sliced (for garnish)

Caramelize the onions in the olive oil for 20 minutes at medium high in a large soup pot. Stir frequently.
Add the rest of the ingredients except sour cream and green onions.
Cover and bring to a boil.
Reduce heat to simmer for about 1 hour.
Serve steaming hot in heated chili bowls.
Top with a tablespoon of sour cream.
Garnish with a few slices of green onions.
Serves 4
Approximately 363 calories per serving with sour cream.

Cold Day! Hot Chili!

Speaking of comfort foods, there is nothing more comforting than a wonderful bowl
of butternut squash soup. It's rich and creamy and good to the last bite!

Incredibly Delicious!
Butternut Squash Soup

1   tablespoon butter
2   cups butternut squash, peeled, cubed into ½ inch pieces
1   cup Yukon Gold potato, peeled and cubed into ½ inch pieces
1   sweet onion, roughly chopped
2   cups low sodium chicken broth (see product page)
½   cup half and half cream
1   teaspoon nutmeg
½   teaspoon cinnamon
Freshly ground pepper
Pinch Kosher salt
Fresh cilantro (for garnish)

Melt butter in a large heavy saucepan and sauté onion over low heat for 20 minutes. Add
butternut squash and potato cubes. Sauté 5 minutes.
Stir in chicken broth, salt, pepper, nutmeg and cinnamon.
Bring to a boil and then immediately reduce heat, cover and simmer 20 minutes, stirring
occasionally. Purée soup using an electric immersion blender.
Stir in half and half.
Garnish with cilantro and serve *hot* in heated soup bowls.
Serves 4

This is wonderful served with gruyere toasts.
Use a French bread baguette, slice off 8 pieces diagonally and arrange bread slices on baking
sheet. Sprinkle evenly with 2 ounces gruyere cheese, finely grated.
Broil the bread slices 2 minutes until golden. Serve 2 to each guest as accompaniment to the
soup.

Approximately 163 calories per serving for soup.
(Add 100 calories for 2 gruyere toasts).

Split peas, sherry and garlic combine to give this soup irresistible flavor! It's hearty enough to make a great supper when served with a tossed green salad. Top with house made garlic croutons for a delicious accent!

Split Pea Soup with House Made Garlic Croutons

1¼ cup dried green split peas, picked over, rinsed, and drained

4 cups low sodium chicken broth (see product page)

1 large sweet onion, coarsely chopped

2 tablespoons extra virgin olive oil

2 carrots sliced into ¼ inch rounds

3 cloves garlic, minced

1 cup dry sherry

1 tablespoon fresh thyme leaves

½ teaspoon red pepper flakes

¼ teaspoon celery seeds

1 bay leaf

Freshly ground pepper

Freshly made croutons for garnish (see Caesar Salad for recipe)

Caramelize onions in oil at medium high temperature for 20 minutes in a 4 quart soup pan. Stir frequently.

Add carrots and garlic and then sauté for another 5 minutes.

Add the split peas, broth, sherry, thyme, pepper flakes, celery seeds and the bay leaf.

Bring to a boil and then reduce to simmer for 60 minutes. Let cool.

Remove the bay leaf and purée with an electric immersion blender, leaving a small amount of texture.

Reheat until steaming hot and serve in heated soup bowls.

Serves 4

Approximately 343 calories per serving with croutons.

Split Pea Soup with House Made Garlic Croutons

Oyster lovers will love this oyster stew!
Simple to prep, easy to make, and delicious to eat!

The World's Best Oyster Stew!

4   cups extra-small fresh oysters, shucked
2   tablespoons unsalted butter
4   cups half and half cream
½ cup fresh dill, chopped (reserve for garnish)

Heat half and half in a soup pan at medium. Do not allow to boil. Add oysters. Leave oysters in heated half and half for 5 minutes.

Put soup in 4 heated soup bowls. Top each serving with ½ tablespoon butter and garnish with freshly chopped dill. Serve piping hot immediately.

Serves 4
Approximately 277 calories per serving.

The World's Best Oyster Stew!

Santa Fe is a foodies Mecca! One of our favorite Santa Fe dishes is this Chicken, Bean and Vegetable Soup. Served steaming hot, it's absolutely delicious on a cold winter night. Beans are a healthy choice, containing 6-7 grams of fiber per ½ cup.

Santa Fe Chicken, Bean and Vegetable Soup

2   chicken breasts (about 7 ounces each), boneless and skinless, cubed
1   tablespoon extra virgin olive oil
1   sweet onion, chopped
2   carrots, sliced in ¼ inch rounds
1   zucchini, sliced in ½ inch rounds
2   stalks celery, cut in ¼ inch slices
2   cloves garlic, minced
1   jalapeño pepper, finely sliced and diced
1   tablespoon chili powder
1   tablespoon cumin
¼   teaspoon cinnamon

¼   teaspoon ancho chili pepper spice (ground)
½   teaspoon fresh ground black pepper
2   cups low sodium chicken broth (see product page)
1   cup dry sherry
2   tablespoons lemon juice
1   cup chopped tomatoes (see product page)
2   cups mixed dried beans, (northern, pinto, lima beans, or other)

Wash the beans and pick over. Soak overnight in cold water. Drain.
Transfer beans to large soup pot with fresh water.
Cook covered at medium heat about 1 hour. Drain & reserve beans.
Caramelize onions in olive oil at medium high for 20 minutes. Stir often.
Add carrots, zucchini, celery, jalapeño and garlic and sauté 10 minutes.
Combine spices with broth, sherry and lemon juice. Whisk and add to pot.
Add cubed chicken and chopped tomatoes to pot.
Bring to a boil, covered. Then reduce heat to simmer. Cook for 2 hours.
Add beans and reheat. Serve piping hot in pre-heated soup plates.
A glass of New Zealand Sauvignon Blanc and a loaf of sourdough bread to make this a great one course supper.
Serves 4
Approximately 371 calories per serving.
(Bread and wine not included in calorie count!)

This sweet and sour soup will become a favorite for your family too! This is a great dinner to enjoy on a cold winter evening. Not only is it absolutely delicious, it is fat free, low calorie and very good for you!

Cabbage Borscht

26 ounce chicken breasts, boneless and skinless, cubed
1   head white cabbage, sliced and chopped (or ½ red and white)
2   large sweet onions, chopped
3   cups chopped tomatoes (see product page)
2   fresh tomatoes, chopped
1   cup vermouth
½   cup lemon juice
4   cups water
3   tablespoons brown sugar
3   tablespoons Heinz chili sauce
¼   cup balsamic vinegar
Worcestershire sauce, dash
3   tablespoons Dijon mustard
2   bay leaves
2   tablespoons caraway seeds
1   bunch fresh oregano, chopped

Caramelize onions in olive oil for 20 minutes at medium high heat in a large ovenproof soup pan. Stir frequently. Add all other ingredients. Bring to a boil on top of the stove, then put in preheated 350 degree oven and bake for 2 hours. Serve in heated soup plates.
Serves 4
Approximately 360 calories per serving.

TIPS FROM THE CHEFS: Another way to make this soup is to substitute beef for the chicken. Use 1½ pound of chuck roast, remove all visible fat, and cut it into 2 inch cubes.
This gives you a wonderful recipe that the beef eaters in your family will love!

Main Event

Hickory Smoked Fresh Wild Caught Salmon on Plank 99

Pan Sautéed Fresh Wild Caught Salmon 101

Poached Fresh Wild Caught Salmon, Lemon and Dill 102

Pepper Crusted Halibut with a Lemon Twist 103

Steamer Clams with Garlic, Butter and Vermouth 105

Swordfish to Die For… 107

Pan Sautéed Sand Dabs with Fresh Lemon 108

Petrale Sole Pan Sautéed with Almonds 109

Caramelized Onion, Aged Cheddar, Fresh Dill Frittata 111

Smoked Salmon, Caramelized Onion, Chive Frittata 112

Smoked Salmon Hash with Caramelized Onions 113

Five Star Cuisine Garlic Chicken and Spicy
Fettuccine with Lemon and Goat Cheese

Herb Roasted Rack of Lamb

**Rack of Lamb…if you *love* lamb you will find our 2 favorite recipes irresistible.
Either one will make a very special entrée for good friends and special guests.**

Roasted Rack of Lamb, Two Ways!

The photo shows the herb roasted rack, but we also love the honey ginger recipe, so try one now and the other another time. Both recipes require two 8 bone racks of lamb for 4 people, all visible fat removed. Ask your butcher to do this for you (you may have to do extra trimming at home).

Marinade #1 Fresh Thyme, Oregano, Rosemary and Garlic

2 tablespoons extra virgin olive oil	2 tablespoons chopped fresh thyme
2 tablespoons chopped fresh rosemary	2 cloves of garlic, minced finely
2 tablespoons chopped fresh oregano	2 tablespoons freshly cracked pepper

Marinade #2 Honey, Soy Sauce, Garlic, and Ginger

4 tablespoons honey	6 cloves of garlic, minced finely
4 tablespoons light soy sauce	2 tablespoons fresh ginger, peeled and minced finely

Combine all ingredients and apply either marinade to all sides of lamb racks. Put racks in a ceramic dish, cover with plastic wrap and store in the refrigerator for 4 hours. One hour prior to roasting remove from the refrigerator and allow to come to room temperature.

Preheat oven to 400 degrees.
Place racks of lamb in oven for 20 minutes.
Insert instant meat thermometer in thickest part of lamb.
When meat thermometer reads 125 degrees, remove from oven.
Let rack rest for 10 minutes on carving board so juices will rise in meat which should be pink (medium rare) when cut. Cut racks in half and serve.
Serves 4
Approximately 415 calories per serving for either recipe.

So tender you can cut it with a spoon!
This incredible lamb dish is inspired by the extraordinary bistros of France.
For a memorable experience, serve it with creamed spinach, pureed yams, and a good pinot noir!

Seven Hour Lamb

4   pound leg of lamb, bone in, all visible fat removed
3   large sweet onions, peeled and chopped
Leaves from 4 stems of fresh rosemary
8   cloves of garlic, minced
3   tablespoons coarse freshly ground pepper

Rub leg of lamb with minced garlic. Liberally sprinkle rosemary and freshly ground pepper over all sides of lamb.
Put the chopped onions in the bottom of a heavy Dutch oven.
Place leg of lamb on the bed of onions and cover.
Put Dutch oven in preheated 250 degree oven.
Roast 7 hours with the lid on until meat is ready to fall off the bone.
Serve lamb on large serving platter and invite your guests to scoop out their own lamb from the leg onto warm dinner plates.
Serves 4
Approximately 440 calories per serving based on average 6 ounce serving.

Our favorite dinner in Vienna is Taffelspitz. It's a simple braised dish which becomes an elegant dinner entrée at one of the great restaurants of Vienna when accompanied by amazing Austrian potatoes.

Brisket of Beef with Creamed Horseradish Sauce

2 pounds brisket, visible fat trimmed
Low sodium beef broth, enough to cover the beef
1 sweet onion, roughly chopped
2 carrots, sliced into ½ inch rounds
1 leek, finely chopped
2 cloves garlic, minced
3 stalks of celery, sliced into ¼ inch slices
1 bay leaf
1 teaspoon ground allspice
3 tablespoons unsalted butter (1 for vegetables, 2 for potatoes)

To make brisket:
Sauté onions, carrots, leek, and garlic in 1 tablespoon butter in
Dutch oven with lid. Add brisket and cover with broth.
Braise slowly for 3 hours at 275 degrees, until meat is fork tender.

To make horseradish sauce:
¼ cup horseradish
1 cup whipping cream
Whip the cream until it peaks, then add horseradish and chill until ready to serve.

To make Austrian potatoes:
3 Yukon Gold potatoes
Dice potatoes. Melt 2 tablespoons unsalted butter in 10 inch fry pan.
Sauté potatoes 30 minutes at medium high until brown and crispy.

Serve brisket, potatoes, and vegetables on heated dinner plates.
Serves 4
Approximately 850 calories per serving including horseradish sauce and Austrian potatoes.

Amazing Beef Burgundy…French Bistro Style!

Put the "comfort" back into comfort food. Enjoy this Beef Burgundy adapted from the recipe of a wonderful French bistro in Paris! This unforgettable dish is one you'll want to enjoy time and time again! Serve with Crispy Oven Roasted Rosemary Potatoes and a bottle of Pinot Noir for a truly memorable dinner.

Amazing Beef Burgundy...French Bistro Style!

1½ pounds beef chuck roast, visible fat removed, cut into 1 inch cubes
1 tablespoon extra virgin olive oil
2 sweet onions, sliced, diced
4 shallots, diced
8 cloves garlic, minced
4 carrots, sliced in ½ inch rounds
1 cup low sodium chicken broth (see product page)

4 cups red wine
1 orange cut into small cubes
Zest of same orange
2 tablespoons Dijon mustard
1 tablespoon demi-glace (see product page)
2 tablespoons fresh rosemary
2 tablespoons fresh thyme
4 cloves
8 fresh mushrooms, quartered
Freshly ground black pepper

Marinate beef in wine for 4 hours or overnight.
Preheat oven to 275 degrees.
Brown beef on all sides in olive oil for 10 minutes.
Simmer onions, shallots and minced garlic in a Dutch oven for 10 minutes on stovetop.
Add browned beef, sliced carrots, chicken broth and wine and simmer for 10 minutes.
Add orange zest, orange cubes, Dijon mustard, demi-glace, rosemary, thyme, cloves, and pepper and cover.
Braise in oven at 275 degrees for 3 hours, liquid covering meat and vegetables.
Add mushrooms to Dutch oven 10 minutes before serving.
Serve beef, vegetables, and pan juices in heated soup plates.
Serves 4
Approximately 745 calories per serving.

Braised Beef Short Ribs. This recipe is from Marché Restaurant and Bar in Eugene, Oregon. Marché is one of the finest restaurants in the Pacific Northwest, founded by Stephanie Pearl Kimmel, a leader in the development of fine dining in the Northwest. We love this restaurant and highly recommend it to you. Stephanie's first restaurant in Eugene was The Excelsior Café, opened in 1972, pioneering the use of seasonal menus celebrating the bounty of the region, much as Alice Waters did in Berkeley at Chez Panisse. The Excelsior has been featured in many publications including Food & Wine, Gourmet, and Sunset. In 1997 she opened the French bistro-inspired Marché. In 1998 Stephanie hired Rocky Maselli to be chef de cuisine for Marché. Rocky continues Stephanie's tradition of working with local farmers to bring seasonal regional menus to Marché. In 2006 Stephanie was nominated for a richly deserved James Beard award.

Marché Restaurant and Bar

296 E. 5th Avenue, in the Historic Fifth Street Market, Eugene Oregon.

Phone 541 342 3612

www.marcherestaurant.com/menus.htm

Braised Beef Short Ribs from
Marché Restaurant

Braised Beef Short Ribs
Recipe from Marché Restaurant

12 beef short ribs, cut about 2 inches thick, visible fat trimmed
2   large yellow onions, peeled and roughly chopped
2   large carrots, peeled and roughly chopped
½   head celery, cleaned and roughly chopped
4   cloves garlic, peeled and minced
4   sprigs fresh rosemary
4   sprigs fresh thyme
2   cups red wine
2   cups beef stock
3   bay leaves
Freshly ground pepper (a generous amount)
½   cup fresh parsley, washed and chopped (reserve for garnish)

Season the short ribs with Kosher salt and pepper. Put short ribs in glass or porcelain bowl, add herbs and wine.
Marinate overnight in refrigerator.
Preheat oven to 475 degrees. Remove short ribs from marinade.
Place bone side down on a sheet pan. Brown 10 minutes (reserve wine).
Place vegetables on the bottom of a large Dutch oven. Place short ribs on top of vegetables.
Add reserved wine and 2 cups beef stock to cover ribs. Cover dish tightly.
Reduce temperature to 350 degrees. Begin braising in oven.
After 1 hour, check for doneness. Ribs are done when meat is almost falling off the bones (Approximately 2 hours).
Remove from oven and pour off braising liquid (reserve).
Increase temperature to 475 degrees.
Pour reserved braising liquid over ribs. Reheat until piping hot.
Serve with horseradish mashed potatoes (See recipe in SideKicks).
Serves 4
Approximately 675 calories per serving.

Five Star Cuisine Garlic Chicken

This is one of our signature dishes! If you like garlic, you'll love this dish! We first tasted this in a bistro in Paris years ago. We fell in love with garlic chicken! It meets all of our essential criteria…simple to prepare, healthy, and delicious!

Five Star Cuisine Garlic Chicken

4   chicken breasts, boneless and skinless, about 6 ounces each
1   tablespoon extra virgin olive oil
2   tablespoons unsalted butter (reserve 1 for sauce)
10 garlic cloves cut in half (20 flat half-cloves of garlic)
Juice of 2 freshly squeezed lemons
¼ cup dry vermouth
Fresh ground black pepper

Heat oil and butter in a large skillet.
Wash and dry chicken breasts and sprinkle liberally with cracked pepper.
Sear chicken for 5 minutes each side at medium high.
Remove chicken breasts from the pan and set aside.
Place garlic half-cloves in remaining oil and butter in pan. Sauté 5 minutes at medium-high heat, turning to get brown on both sides.
Return chicken breasts to pan, placing them on top of the garlic cloves and sauté, covered, at low heat for 10 minutes.
To serve, remove chicken breasts from pan and place on heated plates.
Place 5 garlic half-cloves on top of each breast.
Add dry vermouth, 1 tablespoon butter and lemon juice to the pan.
Turn heat to high and reduce pan juices to thicken.
Pour pan juices over chicken.
Serves 4
Approximately 330 calories per serving.

TIPS FROM THE CHEFS: *Garlic is very healthy for you! An ounce of garlic supplies more than 15% of your daily requirement of vitamin C plus it is high in B6 and tryptophan! It's also a natural antibiotic. (from caloriecount.about.com)*

Crispy Roast Chicken with Rosemary, Garlic and Lemon

Crispy Roast Chicken becomes a very special dinner at our home!
It is one of the most mouthwatering chicken dishes you will ever taste!

Crispy Roast Chicken with Rosemary, Garlic and Lemon

4   pound fryer chicken, wing tips and tail cut off, all visible fat removed
3   tablespoons olive oil
Juice of 2 lemons
3   garlic cloves, minced
Herbs of Provence,(see product page)
Freshly ground pepper

Rub chicken with olive oil inside and out and squeeze lemon juice over it.
Sprinkle black pepper and Herbs of Provence liberally over chicken.
Place chicken on a rack, breast side up, in a large roasting pan.
Roast for 1 hour and 15 minutes in preheated 400 degree oven.
Chicken is done when brown and crisp (internal temperature 175 degrees).
Remove chicken and place on wood carving board for 15 minutes.
To serve, quarter the chicken and place one quarter on each plate.
Garnish with freshly chopped parsley.
Serves 4
Approximately 377 calories per serving.

Chef Bob Carving the Chicken while his
Brother Gary Checks it Out!

Fill your heaviest Dutch oven with these great ingredients and cook them very slowly.
Enjoy the wonderful smells from the kitchen and prepare for a feast!

Braised Chicken with Parsnips, Carrots and Yam

2   sweet onions, chopped fine
3   tablespoons extra-virgin olive oil (2 for
     sautéing onions and 1 for searing chicken)
4   chicken legs and 4 chicken thighs,
     visible fat removed
2   carrots, peeled and sliced into ½ inch rounds
2   parsnips, peeled and sliced into ½ inch rounds
1   yam, peeled and sliced into ½ inch rounds
3   cloves of garlic, finely minced

1   tablespoon fresh oregano leaves
1   teaspoon Herbs of Provence
     (see product page)
1   teaspoon turmeric
2   bay leaves
5   whole cloves
     Freshly ground black pepper
2   cups low sodium chicken broth
     (see product page)
2   cups dry sherry

Caramelize sweet onions in 2 tablespoons olive oil in the Dutch oven for 20 minutes at medium-high heat or until they start to turn brown. Stir frequently.

Remove onions and set aside.

Meanwhile, pre-heat oven to 400 degrees.

Brown the chicken on each side in olive oil in the Dutch oven.

Spread minced garlic over chicken pieces.

Add caramelized onions, carrots and parsnips.

Pour chicken broth and sherry in a small bowl and add cloves, bay leaves, oregano, Herbs of Provence, turmeric, and black pepper.

Pour liquid over chicken and vegetables to barely cover chicken and vegetables. They need to be covered with liquid while braising.

Place Dutch oven, covered, in your oven at 400 degrees for 30 minutes.

Then reduce to 275 degrees and braise for 1 hour, covered.

Add yam and braise 1 more hour. Check periodically.

Add more sherry if needed. Serve in heated soup bowls.

Serves 4

Approximately 470 calories per serving.

Everyone raves about our chicken cooked for 4 hours in the Dutch oven.
The meat falls off the bone!

Four Hour Braised Chicken with Garlic and Rosemary

4 pound fryer chicken, wing tips and tail cut off and all visible fat removed
2 sweet onions, chopped
2 tablespoons extra virgin olive oil (1 for onions, 1 for browning chicken)
3 cloves garlic, minced finely
½ cup fresh rosemary, chopped
   Freshly ground black pepper

Caramelize onions in olive oil in Dutch oven, about 20 minutes at medium heat, stirring frequently.
Rub chicken with olive oil and minced garlic.
Put rosemary all over outside and inside cavity of chicken.
Sprinkle liberally with fresh ground pepper.
Position chicken over chopped onions, breast side up.
Cover and braise in preheated oven at 275 degrees.
for 4 hours. Serve on heated dinner plates.
Serves 4
Approximately 400 calories per serving.

Our Favorite Sunday Night Supper

One of our all time favorite dishes is "Joe's Special," made famous by San Francisco's legendary Italian restaurant, Vanessi's (sadly, no longer in business). Here is an updated version of this classic. Healthier, less fat, fewer calories...and a great one dish supper!

Our Favorite Sunday Night Supper

1 pound freshly ground turkey
2 large sweet onions, chopped
4 bunches spinach, washed very thoroughly
20 large firm crimini mushrooms, sliced
1 large shallot, sliced
1 jalapeño, seeded, chopped
6 large cloves garlic, chopped
2 tablespoons extra virgin olive oil

1 tablespoon Worcestershire sauce
6 dashes of Tabasco
1 tablespoon cumin
2 tablespoons chili powder
1 tablespoon garam masala (see product page)
2 tablespoons fresh oregano, chopped
1 teaspoon freshly ground black pepper
2 tablespoons freshly grated Parmigiano Reggiano cheese (for garnish)

Caramelize onions in olive oil for 20 minutes in a sauté pan at medium-high heat, stirring frequently. Set aside.

Sauté mushrooms, shallot, jalapeño, and garlic for 5 minutes until softened. Set aside.

Put turkey in a bowl. Add cumin, chili powder, garam masala, oregano, pepper, Tabasco and Worcestershire sauces. Set aside.

Cook spinach in boiling water 3 minutes, drain well. Chop spinach and set aside.

Sauté seasoned turkey for 5 minutes. As it gets done, break it up into little pieces using spatula to separate pieces.

Add spinach, onions, garlic, shallot, jalapeño, and mushrooms to turkey and stir fry, tossing all ingredients together until very hot.

Serve on heated plates. Sprinkle freshly grated cheese over top.

Serves 4

Approximately 325 calories per person.

If you crave an explosion of flavors bursting in your mouth, you will love this extraordinary dish. This delightful chutney combined with the zesty chicken creates a perfect marriage. It's healthy, low calorie and simply delicious!

Ginger Chicken with Fresh Mango and Mint Chutney

4 boneless and skinless chicken breasts
1 tablespoon sesame oil

Marinade:
2 tablespoons sesame oil
2 tablespoons fresh ginger, finely chopped
2 cloves garlic, minced

Freshly ground pepper
$\frac{1}{8}$ teaspoon red pepper flakes

Place chicken in a shallow dish.
Combine marinade ingredients and pour over chicken, tossing to coat.
Cover with freshly ground pepper. Cover and chill several hours.
Heat sesame oil in a large skillet over medium high heat.
Pan sauté chicken at medium heat 7 minutes. Turn, cover, and sauté 6 minutes more.

Combine these ingredients for Mango Chutney:
1 teaspoon ground cumin
1 large fresh mango, chopped
(see YouTube videos for how to cut)
$\frac{1}{3}$ cucumber, peeled, seeds removed, and chopped
½ cup chopped red onion

2 teaspoons fresh jalapeno, seeds removed, minced
3 tablespoons fresh lime juice
3 tablespoons mint leaves, thinly sliced
$\frac{1}{8}$ teaspoon coriander
3 tablespoons chopped cilantro

Serves 4
Approximately 371 calories for both chicken and chutney per serving.

TIPS FROM THE CHEFS: *To prepare fresh ginger, peel by scraping skin off with a spoon, slice off all outside surfaces leaving hard stringy core, and then finely chop ginger.*

Our favorite stir-fry...bar none! The secret is in the sauce!
Perfect for a one dish meal. P.S. Don't forget the chop sticks!

Hot and Spicy Szechwan Chicken Stir-Fry

4   chicken breasts (about 6 ounces each), boneless and skinless, cubed
8   fresh shiitake mushrooms, ¼ inch slices
3   green onions, ½ inch diced, cut at 45 degree angle
12 spears asparagus, peeled, and cut at a 45 degree angle

1   red pepper, sliced and diced
1   can water chestnuts, sliced
¼ cup unsalted peanuts
8   ounces snow peas, crisp and firm, ends removed

Ingredients for Szechwan sauce:
3   tablespoons sesame oil
1   tablespoon chili oil
1   tablespoon sweet chili sauce
½ cup dry sherry
2   tablespoons fresh ginger, minced
3   cloves garlic, minced

1   tablespoon light soy sauce
1   tablespoon Chinese 5 spice powder
1   tablespoon brown sugar
1   tablespoon toasted sesame seeds
1   jalapeño, seeds removed, sliced, and diced

Add 2 tablespoons sauce to heated wok. Stir fry chicken for 5 minutes and set aside.
Stir fry mushrooms, asparagus, green onions, red pepper, and water chestnuts, each separately in 1 additional tablespoon sauce, 1 minute.
Set aside. Add rest of sauce to wok. Add back previously cooked chicken, add peanuts and stir fry until steaming hot, Add snow peas and previously stir fried mushrooms, green onions, red pepper, and water chestnuts and stir fry another minute.
Serve immediately on heated dinner plates.
Serves 4
Approximately 547 calories per serving.

Spicy Fettuccine with Lemon and Goat Cheese

This is one of the most exceptional pasta dishes we have ever experienced.
Try it, you will find it irresistible! Serve this dish with our Five Star Cuisine
Garlic Chicken or with a green salad for a lighter dinner!

Spicy Fettuccine with Lemon and Goat Cheese

8   ounces best quality fettuccine
1   pinch of kosher salt (for cooking pasta)
2   tablespoons extra virgin olive oil
2   tablespoons unsalted butter
1   sweet red onion, chopped
1   teaspoon red pepper flakes
1   sweet red pepper, sliced ½ inch
Juice of 2 lemons
Zest of 2 lemons
2   ounces crumbled goat cheese
½   cup fresh cilantro, chopped (reserve for garnish)

Heat olive oil in 10 inch sauté pan.
Sauté chopped onions, red pepper flakes and sweet red pepper slices for 12 minutes at medium
high temperature. Add the butter to onion, red pepper sauce and allow it to melt. Add the
lemon juice and lemon zest to onion red pepper sauce. Heat until steaming. Then reduce heat to
simmer. Cover pan and simmer while pasta cooks.

Bring 3 quarts of water to a boil with a pinch of kosher salt. Put pasta into boiling water (follow
directions on package for time). When fettuccine is "al dente" remove from water and drain.

Put onion red pepper sauce in heated serving bowl. Add crumbled goat cheese.
Add fettuccine to onion red pepper sauce and toss.
Serve immediately on heated plates. Garnish with chopped cilantro.
Serves 4
Approximately 390 calories per serving.

Bouillabaisse

We first experienced bouillabaisse while visiting Marseille, where we fell in love
with a steaming bowl of luscious seafood and broth. It takes longer to make than any
other recipe in this book, but when you taste it, you will say it was worth it!

Bouillabaisse
Clams, Shrimp, Cod, and Scallops in a Heavenly Broth!

2 leeks, minced finely (cut in half
   lengthwise, rinse out any dirt)

1 red bell pepper, cubed

2 oranges (remove zest, set aside,
   peel and cube oranges, set aside)

4 cloves garlic, minced

1 sweet onion, chopped

3 fresh carrots grated

Sauté the above ingredients 15 minutes in 2 tablespoons olive oil in a soup pot:

Add 2 cups chopped tomatoes (see product page)

4 ounces clam broth

2 cups of dry sherry with the dry
   ingredients below mixed in:

2 cups low sodium chicken broth
   (see product page)

1½ teaspoons cumin, 2 bay leaves, 1 tablespoon paprika, 1½ teaspoons fennel seed, 1½ teaspoons
sage, 1 teaspoon coriander, 4 teaspoons basil, ¼ teaspoon cayenne, and pinch of saffron threads
(see product page)

Cook for 50 minutes, covered, at medium temperature.

Add the seafood:

16 manila clams, live, in shell (wrap in
   wet towel to store in refrigerator
   until added to soup)

1 pound white fish (ling cod or any
   other white fish), cut into 2 inch cubes

16 large shrimp (12-15 count),
   shelled and deveined

4 large scallops, cut into quarters

Increase the temperature to medium-high. When the broth begins to boil, add the fish and
shellfish and cook 3-4 minutes until clam shells open and shrimp turns pink.

Place 1 thick slice of sourdough bread in each heated soup bowl and spoon bouillabaisse over
bread. Be sure each serving gets an equal quantity of each kind of seafood.
Garnish with chopped cilantro and serve at once.
Serves 4
Approximately 453 calories per serving.

Garlic Prawns with Red Peppers and Fettuccine

This is our version of a famous dish served in the finest trattorias in Florence and Venice. We loved it in Italy…you will love it at home! Simple and easy to make, and absolutely delicious!

Garlic Prawns with Red Peppers and Fettuccine

8   ounces best quality dried fettuccine
16 large shrimp (12-15 to the pound), shelled, deveined and dried
4   tablespoons unsalted butter
1   sweet red pepper, sliced and diced
1   shallot, finely chopped
3   garlic cloves, minced
Juice of 2 lemons, freshly squeezed
Zest of 2 lemons
½   cup dry vermouth
2   tablespoons fresh dill, finely chopped (reserve for garnish)

Saute shallot and garlic in butter for 2-3 minutes.
Add shrimp and sauté 3-4 minutes until they turn pink.
Remove shrimp from shallot & garlic and set aside.
Add vermouth, lemon juice, lemon zest, and red pepper and simmer.
Meanwhile cook fettuccine according to package directions.
When done, drain and reserve in heated bowl.
Bring shallot, red pepper, garlic, and lemon mixture to a boil and toss fettuccine with mixture.
Serve on heated dinner plates, putting equal quantities of fettuccine on each plate. Arrange 4 shrimp over fettuccine on each plate.
Garnish with fresh dill.
Serves 4
Approximately 467 calories per serving.

Pan Seared Sea Scallops. This recipe is from Restaurant Beck, one of the finest restaurants in the Pacific Northwest! Justin Wills, Chef/Owner, has been executive chef at fine restaurants from coast to coast, including the famed Bay House restaurant in Lincoln City, Oregon. He trained at the Culinary Institute of America in Hyde Park, N.Y. Restaurant Beck is located within the Whale Cove Inn, a new luxury hotel in Depoe Bay on the beautiful Oregon central coast. Beck offers marvelous New American cuisine. We loved Beck so much we wanted to recommend it to you. We are excited to include one of Justin's recipes in our book. Here is what one guest wrote after dining at Beck. "Beck boasts a wonderful view of Whale Cove. The food was amazing. The menu is based on fresh local organic ingredients. My wife had cinnamon smoked duck while I had the lamb loin with a blackberry sauce. I will drive from Portland just to have a meal at Beck and smile all the way to and from." (L. Cameron, Portland, Oregon.) He gave it 5 stars. We agree.

Restaurant Beck

2345 SW Highway 101, Depoe Bay, Oregon. Phone 541 765 3220.

To see a photo of the Pan Seared Sea Scallops and the incredible view from the restaurant go to www.restaurantbeck.com.

View of the Whale Cove Inn,
Home of Restaurant Beck

Pan Seared Sea Scallops
Recipe from Restaurant Beck

1 pound fresh tomatoes (beefsteak or hothouse)
1 tablespoon kosher salt

8 large sea scallops
1 cup cantaloupe melon, ¼ inch diced
2 teaspoons jalapeño, seeded and minced
28 celery leaves
4 teaspoons lemon juice
1 tablespoon extra virgin olive oil
1 teaspoon unsalted butter (for searing scallops)
1 teaspoon vegetable oil (for searing scallops)

To make tomato water: Rough chop tomatoes. Place chopped tomatoes and salt into a blender. Blend until smooth. Line a fine mesh sieve with cheese cloth and pour in pureed tomatoes. Tomato "water" will <u>slowly</u> drip out. It is best to do this the night before.

In a bowl combine melon, celery leaves, jalapeño, lemon juice, olive oil, and a dash of salt and pepper. Add 4 tablespoons of tomato water. Toss to combine.

Place melon mixture into 4 small individual serving bowls.

Season scallops with a touch of salt and pepper and sear in one teaspoon of butter and one teaspoon of vegetable oil over medium high heat until caramelized on one side.
Turn scallops over and place in a 350 degree pre-heated oven for one minute.

Top each serving bowl of melon mixture with two seared sea scallops, brown side up. Serve on heated plates. Enjoy!
Serves 4
Approximately 160 calories per serving.

Hickory Smoked Fresh Wild Caught Salmon on the Plank

An amazing preparation of wild caught salmon, simple to prep, easy
to cook and worthy of rave reviews.

Hickory Smoked Fresh Wild Caught Salmon on the Plank

1 side of fresh wild caught salmon, about 20 ounces, skin on
2 tablespoons extra virgin olive oil
1 tablespoon Dijon mustard
1 tablespoon brown sugar
2 tablespoons lemon juice
1 lemon, quartered
4 tablespoons freshly chopped dill (for garnish)
1 large wood plank (either alder or cedar), soaked in water 1 hour
½ cup hickory wood chips, soaked in water 20 minutes

Drain wood chips and put in a small pocket of aluminum foil.
Heat the grill to 500 degrees.
Place foil pocket on top of the grate over flame.
Squeeze a generous amount of lemon juice over entire salmon filet.
Spread mustard and brown sugar evenly over salmon.
Turn off the burners on one side of the grill leaving one burner on under wood chip packet.
Lightly sprinkle olive oil on top of the plank.
Place salmon on the plank, skin side down.
Place on the grates and close lid.
Smoke salmon for exactly 13 minutes. No need to turn over.
Garnish with chopped dill. Serve on heated plates with lemon quarters.
Serves 4
Approximately 370 calories per serving.

TIPS FROM THE CHEFS: *Be sure to buy fresh (not previously frozen) wild caught salmon. Farm raised salmon is not the same! Chinook is the best because it is the richest, but sockeye or silver salmon are also very good. During the summer salmon season you can buy wild caught salmon sides at a great price at Costco.*

Pan Sautéed Fresh Wild Caught Salmon

Fresh wild caught salmon from the cold rivers and oceans of the Pacific Northwest is not only one of the world's great delicacies but it's so good for you! It's loaded with heart-healthy Omega 3!

Pan Sautéed Fresh Wild Caught Salmon

4 filets of fresh wild caught salmon, 6 ounces each
2 tablespoons extra virgin olive oil (1 for fish, 1 for pan)
4 tablespoons fresh dill, freshly chopped
Freshly ground black pepper

Grind black pepper liberally over both sides of salmon.
Sprinkle 1 tablespoon olive oil lightly over fish.
Refrigerate until ready to cook.
Add 1 tablespoon of olive oil to 10 inch fry pan. Heat pan to high.
Put salmon in the pan and sear for 1 minute.
Turn fish and sear on other side for 1 minute.
Reduce heat to medium and cook covered 6 minutes on each side.
Serve on heated plates. Garnish salmon with freshly chopped dill.
Serve with freshly cut lemon wedges. Serves 4

Approximately 360 calories per serving.

TIPS FROM THE CHEFS: *Be sure to buy fresh (not previously frozen) wild caught salmon. Farm raised salmon is not the same! Chinook is the best because it is the richest, but sockeye or silver salmon are also very good. During the summer salmon season you can buy wild caught salmon sides at a great price at Costco.*

To enjoy the incredible flavor of fresh wild caught salmon, simply poach it! With a touch of fresh lemon juice…you'll love it! Serve it hot or chilled. Make enough to enjoy chilled for lunch or dinner the next day, perhaps in a Salad Nicoise.

Poached Fresh Wild Caught Salmon with Lemon and Dill

4   filets of fresh wild caught salmon, 6 ounces each
Squeeze of lemon juice
4   tablespoons fresh dill, chopped (for garnish)
2   lemons, quartered

Bring enough water to a boil to cover the fish in a large sauté pan.
Add fish. Reduce temperature to simmer.
Cover the pan and poach filets for exactly 13 minutes.
Serve on warm plates, adding a squeeze of lemon juice and dusting of chopped dill. Serve with freshly cut lemon quarters.
Serves 4
Approximately 300 calories per serving.

TIPS FROM THE CHEFS: *Be sure to buy fresh (not previously frozen) wild caught salmon. Farm raised salmon is not the same! Chinook is the best because it is the richest, but sockeye or silver salmon are also very good. During the summer salmon season you can buy wild caught salmon sides at a great price at Costco.*

When fresh wild halibut is in season, we can't wait to make this delectable dish. We often serve it with garlic spinach. What a treat!

Pepper Crusted Halibut with a Lemon Twist

4   fresh wild halibut filets, approximately 1 inch thick, (6-7 oz each)
2   tablespoons extra virgin olive oil
4   tablespoons lemon juice
Freshly ground black pepper (lots)
4   tablespoons cilantro, finely minced (for garnish)

Rub halibut filets in olive oil and lemon juice. Liberally grind fresh pepper coating on both sides of fish. Use more pepper than you think you should!
Sear both sides of fish for 1 minute at high heat. Then pan sauté, covered, at medium high heat for approximately 5 minutes on each side.
Serve on heated plates. Garnish with freshly chopped cilantro.
Serves 4
Approximately 236 calories per serving.

TIPS FROM THE CHEFS: Fish contains artery-clearing omega-3 fatty acids which not only protect your heart but also your brain. Saturated fats clog arteries that lead to your brain, putting you at risk for stroke while omega-3 fatty acids protect your arteries. They also alter your neurotransmitters and reduce depression! (from realage.com).

Steamer Clams with Garlic, Butter and Vermouth

When Jack Nicholson said "as good as it gets" in the acclaimed Academy Award nominated film, he must have been thinking about these fresh steamer clams in a butter, garlic, and vermouth broth. Enjoy it with sour dough bread and a glass of Oregon pinot gris...um um good!

Steamer Clams with Garlic, Butter and Vermouth

4   pounds fresh steamer clams in shells (approximately 32 clams), washed in cold water
¼   pound butter
3   cloves garlic, finely minced
1   cup dry vermouth
3   tablespoons freshly chopped dill

Melt butter and sauté garlic in a heavy soup pot with a tight fitting lid.
Add vermouth.
Bring liquid to boil, put in clams, bring down to medium heat and cover the pot. Steam clams for 3 minutes and then check to see if the clam shells are open. Steam until all clams open. Add more vermouth if needed.
Remove clams to individual bowls and pour broth equally over clams.
Serve steaming hot in heated soup plates.
Garnish with chopped dill.
Serve with thick slices of sourdough bread for dipping. Enjoy!!!
Serves 4
Approximately 320 Calories Per Serving.

Swordfish to Die for…

Swordfish is incredibly delicious with no fat and half the calories of beef! Just be sure the swordfish is very fresh. Ask at your fish market for a thick, ¾ to 1 inch cut. Serve with Garlic Spinach and Oven Roasted Rosemary Potatoes.

Swordfish to Die for...

4   swordfish filets, ¾ to 1 inch thick, (approximately 6-7 oz each)
2   tablespoons extra virgin olive oil
1   lemon, cut in 4 wedges
Freshly ground black pepper. You can't put on too much pepper!
1   tablespoon fresh dill, chopped finely, (reserve for garnish)

Drizzle olive oil on both sides of fish.
Grind generous amounts of pepper on both sides.
Sear for 1 minute at high heat on both sides.
Pan sauté at medium high heat for approximately 5 minutes each side.
Serve on heated plates.
Garnish with fresh chopped dill. Place a large lemon wedge on each plate.
Serves 4
Approximately 312 calories per serving.

**Sand Dabs are at their best pan sautéed until nicely browned. They are
an excellent choice for a special guest seafood dinner.**

Pan Sautéed Sand Dabs with Fresh Lemon

8   sand dabs (must be fresh, wild caught, not previously frozen)
1   cup buttermilk
1   cup flour
2   fresh lemons, quartered
2   tablespoons butter
½   cup parsley, freshly chopped (for garnish)

Marinate fish in buttermilk for 30 minutes.
Drain buttermilk and dredge fish on both sides in flour.
Pan sauté in a preheated pan at medium temperature for 3 minutes on each side until fish is
nicely browned.
Remove bone from center and place meat on heated plates.
Drizzle 1 teaspoon of melted butter over fish.
Garnish with freshly chopped parsley.
Serve with lemon quarters.
Serves 4
Approximately 387 calories per serving.

TIPS FROM THE CHEFS: *If sand dabs are not available, their cousin, rex sole, is very similar and equally delicious. Prepare
rex sole in exactly the same way as sand dabs.*
*No matter what fish you are buying, the secret to success is wild caught as compared to farm raised, and fresh, not previously
frozen. If the fish you were going to buy is only available previously frozen choose a different fish, or make a different dish!*

Some of the world's finest seafood can be found in the French Quarter in New Orleans. Nothing is more "The Big Easy" than Sole Meunière Almandine at Galatoires! Close your eyes while enjoying our wonderful version of this sole. You will hear the jazz on Bourbon Street floating through the air!

Petrale Sole Pan Sautéed with Almonds

8   filets of boneless petrale sole (approximately 4 ounces each)
½   cup flour
½   cup milk
3   tablespoons unsalted butter (for sautéing fish)
½   cup sliced almonds
1   tablespoon unsalted butter (for sautéing almonds)
1   tablespoon unsalted butter (melted to pour over fish when serving)
½   cup chopped fresh Italian parsley (for garnish)
1   lemon cut into wedges

Sauté sliced almonds in butter until brown and set aside.
Dampen sole in milk, dredge in flour.
Sauté filets in sauté pans at high heat for 2 minutes on each side until brown and crisp.
Serve on heated dinner plates and drizzle melted butter over fish.
Garnish with freshly chopped parsley.
Serve with lemon wedges.
Serves 4
Approximately 497 calories per serving.

TIPS FROM THE CHEFS: *When sautéing fish you need a little room between each piece of fish. You will need 2 10 or 12 inch sauté pans if preparing this recipe for 4.*

Caramelized Onion, Aged Cheddar and Fresh Dill Frittata

For a magnificent Sunday brunch, serve this absolutely delicious frittata.

Caramelized Onion, Aged Cheddar and Fresh Dill Frittata

4 eggs
1 sweet onion, chopped
2 tablespoons extra virgin olive oil (1 tablespoon for onions, 1 for frittata fry pan)
4 tablespoons fresh dill, finely chopped (reserve 2 tablespoons for garnish)
2 ounces 3 year aged cheddar cheese, cubed
1 tablespoon unsalted butter
Cracked black pepper, to taste

Caramelize onions in 1 tablespoon olive oil for 20 minutes at medium heat, stirring frequently. Set aside.
Beat eggs. Add caramelized onion, 2 tablespoons dill, and cheese.
Heat butter and 1 tablespoon oil in a nonstick 10 inch fry pan.
Pour in egg mixture. Cook approximately 5 minutes at medium temperature, lifting edges to allow liquid on top to fill in underneath and frittata to become *almost* solidified.
Meanwhile, place oven rack near broiler element and preheat broiler on high setting. Put the fry pan under broiler, keeping handle out of range of heat, for 30 seconds, or just until frittata liquid is solidified on top and slightly brown.
Slide frittata out of the pan and cut into 2 sections. Serve a section to each person immediately on heated plates.
Garnish with remaining chopped dill.
Serves 2
Approximately 471 calories per serving.

TIPS FROM THE CHEFS: *This recipe is easiest to make for 2 people. If you are serving 4 people. make 2 recipes and cook in 2 10 inch fry pans.*

**This smoked salmon frittata shows off the rich smoky tones of the
salmon punctuated by lively sweet onions and spices.
Our guests rave about this dish!**

Smoked Salmon, Caramelized Onion and Chive Frittata

4 eggs
4 ounces smoked salmon, chopped
1 sweet onion, chopped
1 tablespoon extra virgin olive oil
1 tablespoon unsalted butter
2 tablespoons fresh oregano, fresh, chopped
½ teaspoon red pepper flakes
½ cracked black pepper
1 tablespoon low fat sour cream (for garnish)
1 bunch chives, chopped (for garnish)

Caramelize onions in olive oil for 20 minutes at medium heat, stirring frequently.
Beat eggs. Add caramelized onions, smoked chopped salmon, oregano, and red pepper flakes.
Heat a small amount of butter and 1 tablespoon of oil in a nonstick 10 inch fry pan. Pour in egg
mixture. Cook approximately 5 minutes at medium heat, lifting edges to allow liquid on top to
fill in underneath and frittata to become *almost* solidified.
Meanwhile place oven rack near broiler element and preheat broiler on high setting. Put the fry
pan under broiler, keeping handle out of range of heat, for 30 seconds or just until frittata liquid
is solidified on top and slightly brown.
Slide frittata out of the pan and cut into 2 sections Serve a section to each person immediately
on heated plates. Top each with a dollop of sour cream and a sprinkle of fresh chopped chives.
Serve on heated plates.
Serves 2
Approximately 395 calories per serving.

TIPS FROM THE CHEFS: *This recipe is most successful when made for 2 people. If you are serving 4 people make 2 recipes and
cook in 2 10 inch fry pans.*

When guests or family get a whiff of Smoked Salmon Hash they will be rushing to the table! It's absolutely delicious!

Smoked Salmon Hash with Caramelized Onions

8 ounces best quality smoked salmon, cubed (see tip below)
2 Yukon Gold potatoes, peeled and cut into ½ inch cubes
1 yam, peeled and cut into ½ inch cubes
3 tablespoons unsalted butter
1 tablespoon extra virgin olive oil
1 sweet onion, chopped
Fresh parsley, chopped (for garnish)

Melt butter in large sauté pan and sauté potatoes at medium heat until golden, approximately 30 minutes, stirring frequently.

In a 10 inch fry pan, caramelize onion and garlic in 1 tablespoon olive oil at medium heat for about 20 minutes, stirring frequently.

Combine smoked salmon, potatoes, and onion. Sauté at medium high until hash is crisp and golden, 4-6 minutes.

Serve on heated dinner plates. Garnish with freshly chopped parsley.

Serves 4

TIPS FROM THE CHEFS: Be sure to use your own house smoked salmon or get your salmon at a specialty seafood store that smokes their own fish.

DO NOT buy supermarket smoked salmon…it's just not the same.

SideKicks

French Bistro Lyonnaise Potatoes 116

Incredibly Delicious Creamed Spinach 117

Fresh Spinach Sautéed with Garlic 117

The World's Greatest Potato Cake…Bar None! 118

Horseradish Mashed Potatoes 118
Marché Restaurant

Oven Roasted Rosemary Potatoes 119

Oven Roasted Vegetables 120

Fresh Asparagus with Lemon Beurre Blanc 121

Puréed Yams with Cointreau 121

French Green Beans with Toasted Almonds 122

Garlic Sugar Snap Peas 122

Crispy Garlic Fries 123

Roasted Butternut Squash with Nutmeg and Cloves` 124

Puréed Parsnips 124

Wild Wild Rice with Mushrooms and Sautéed Almonds 125

French Bistro Lyonnaise Potatoes

1 sweet onion, cubed into ½ inch slices
4 russet potatoes, peeled, cut into half inch cubes
1 tablespoon extra virgin olive oil
2 tablespoons unsalted butter
4 cloves garlic, minced

Caramelize onion in olive oil on medium heat for 20 minutes, stirring frequently, until brown.
Remove from fry pan and set aside.
Saute garlic in olive oil until brown and set aside.
Saute potato slices in butter for 20 minutes until browned on both sides.
Add back onions and garlic and toss with potatoes.
Keep hot until ready to serve.
Serves 4
Approximately 210 calories per serving.

French Bistro Lyonnaise Potatoes

Incredibly Delicious Creamed Spinach

A marvelous side dish with lamb, beef, or fish. Add a wonderful potato dish such as Lyonnaise Potatoes and turn a simple dinner into a five star feast!

3 large bunches spinach,
    cleaned thoroughly
2 tablespoons butter

1 tablespoon flour
½ cup half and half cream
½ teaspoon grated nutmeg

Steam spinach 2 minutes until wilted. Drain and chop into a coarse puree.
Melt butter in a 2 quart sauce pan, add flour to butter, and stir until it is smooth. Cook gently for 5 minutes, slowly adding half and half, until sauce thickens and becomes a roux. Remove from heat. Stir in any remaining half and half and the nutmeg. Simmer 2-3 minutes. Set aside.
Stir the chopped spinach into the sauce and simmer until ready to serve.
Serves 4
Approximately 108 calories per serving.

Also great with another spinach variation:

Fresh Spinach Sautéed with Garlic

2 heads fresh spinach, washed and rewashed to rinse out all sand
3 large cloves garlic, finely minced
1 tablespoon olive oil

Put washed spinach in 4 quart sauce pan half full of boiling water.
Reduce heat to medium and let spinach cook about 2 minutes until it wilts.
Remove spinach to colander to drain. Press spinach to remove as much water as possible. Put spinach on chopping board and chop finely.
Heat olive oil in 10 inch sauté pan at medium high.
Sauté garlic in olive oil for 2 minutes.
Add chopped spinach and stir fry until spinach is heated through.
Serves 4
Approximately 42 calories per serving.

The World's Greatest Potato Cake...Bar None!

This recipe is the result of our collaboration with Robert E. Smith, Professor of Economics, University of Oregon, lifelong friend and an exceptionally talented home chef. Over the years, we tested *dozens* of variations before arriving at this recipe which we believe to be the best ever!

2 large russet potatoes, washed, peeled, dried and cut into chunks

4 tablespoons extra-virgin olive oil, 2 for each pan
6 tablespoons unsalted butter, 3 for each pan

Coarsely grate potatoes in food processor. Squeeze moisture out of potatoes with a paper towel.

Preheat 2 non stick 7 inch fry pans on medium heat.
Add 1 tablespoon of oil and 1 ½ tablespoons of butter to each pan.
Put half of grated potatoes into each pan.
Spread out potatoes to fill pans.
Cook for 12 minutes on one side. Bottom should now be nice and brown. Cook a minute or two longer until it is brown.
Slide cake from pan to a plate, crispy side down.
Put 1 tablespoon of oil and 1 ½ tablespoons of butter in each pan again.
Invert plate over pan so cake flips into pan crispy side up. Cook raw side at medium heat for 12 minutes or until crispy brown.
To serve, slide cakes out of pans to heated plates. Cut in half and serve half of a potato cake to each person.
Approximately 320 calories per serving.

Horseradish Mashed Potatoes from Marché Restaurant

2½ pounds yellow fin potatoes or russet potatoes
½ cup milk

3 ounces unsalted butter
Kosher salt and freshly ground pepper
2 tablespoons prepared horseradish

Peel and rinse the potatoes and cut into halves. Place in a large saucepan and cover with cold water and a teaspoon of salt. Bring to a boil and cook until tender, about 20 minutes. Drain thoroughly. Put potatoes through a ricer or mash with a potato masher. Stir in milk and butter until smoothly incorporated. Add grated horseradish and salt and pepper to taste.

Oven Roasted Rosemary Potatoes

One of our favorite potato dishes…so easy to make and such a pleasure to eat!

4   Yukon Gold potatoes, peeled and cut into ½ inch thick rounds
3   tablespoons unsalted butter
Fresh rosemary leaves removed from 4 large sprigs, chopped
Freshly cracked black pepper

Preheat oven to 400 degrees.
Lean potatoes in rows. Melt the butter and drizzle over potatoes.
Sprinkle liberally with fresh chopped rosemary.
Add cracked pepper liberally over potatoes.
Roast for 1 hour uncovered at 400 degrees or until brown and crispy on top. Serve sizzling as the perfect accompaniment to any casual bistro dinner.
Serves 4
Approximately 175 calories per serving.

Rosemary Potatoes Ready to
Roast in the Oven

Oven Roasted Vegetables

Sweet, caramelized and absolutely delicious! Use any winter root vegetables that look good in the market if those listed in the recipe are not available. Root vegetables are excellent sources of Vitamins A and C, Potassium and Fiber.

¼ cup extra virgin olive oil
¼ cup balsamic vinegar
1 large sweet onion, cut in quarters
2 parsnips, peeled and sliced into 1 inch pieces
1 yam, peeled and sliced into 1 inch pieces, cut pieces in half
1 turnip, peeled and sliced into 1 inch pieces, cut pieces in half

1 tablespoon fennel seeds
Fresh ground black pepper
2 carrots, peeled, cut in 1 inch rounds
1 sweet red pepper, cut in large slices
8 whole cloves of garlic, peeled
2 shallots, peeled, cut in half
1 cup cilantro, freshly snipped leaves (reserve for garnish)

Whisk olive oil, balsamic vinegar, fennel seeds and pepper together in large bowl. Add all ingredients and toss thoroughly. Marinate for 30 minutes. Arrange in a large baking dish in one layer if possible.

Roast uncovered at 400 degrees for 30 minutes, then 350 degrees for one hour until vegetables begin to caramelize and turn brown on edges.
Toss occasionally during roasting. Check after 1 hour to determine vegetables are tender.
Serve as a side dish with roasted meat or poultry.
Garnish plates with freshly chopped cilantro.
Serves 4
Approximately 374 calories per serving.

Oven Roasted Vegetables

Fresh Asparagus with Lemon Beurre Blanc
When in season, enjoy asparagus often!
It's so good as a side with fish, chicken, or any meat.

1   pound fresh asparagus, preferably the thicker ones, stalks peeled
     (this makes them very tender to eat)
2   tablespoons unsalted butter
     Juice of 1 lemon

Melt butter and slowly whisk in lemon juice, one drop at a time.
Whisk until all lemon juice has been absorbed into the butter.
Put asparagus spears in 2 cups of boiling water in sauté pan.
Cook at medium high heat for exactly 3 minutes.
Immediately remove asparagus and plunge into ice cold water to stop cooking. Pour sauce over asparagus and serve at once.
Serves 4
Approximately 65 calories per serving.

Puréed Yams with Cointreau
One of our all time favorite dishes and a perfect side with oven roasted turkey.

2   large garnet yams, peeled and cut into 1 inch rounds
1   tablespoon unsalted butter
2   ounces Cointreau

Put yams in boiling water, reduce heat to medium and cook for 7 minutes or until easily pierced with a sharp knife. When done, plunge yams in ice water to stop cooking.
Cut yams in large chunks. Put yams in food processor. Add butter and Cointreau. Pulse for 10 seconds and continue to pulse until yams are the consistency of mashed potatoes.
Put in serving bowl and serve immediately while still hot.
Serves 4
Approximately 82 calories per serving.

French Green Beans with Toasted Almonds
This is a wonderful side dish for any meat, fish, or poultry.

1   pound French green beans (the very skinny ones), stems removed
½   pound sliced raw almonds
2   tablespoons butter (1 for browning almonds, 1 for stir frying green beans & almonds).

Sauté almonds in butter at medium high heat until they begin to brown.
Place green beans in boiling water for 2 minutes. Remove from boiling water and immerse in ice cold water.
Immediately before serving, stir fry green beans with toasted almonds in 1 tablespoon unsalted butter for 1 minute. Serve at once.
Serves 4
Approximately 171 Calories per serving.

Garlic Sugar Snap Peas
An amazing side dish with Chinese food!

1   pound sugar snap peas, washed, and strings removed
1   tablespoon sesame oil
1   tablespoon light soy sauce

Heat sesame oil and soy sauce at medium heat for 3 minutes.
Raise temperature to medium high. Add snap peas and stir fry for 2 minutes.
Serve immediately as a side dish with Asian food but also nice with any meat, fish, or poultry.
Serves 4
Approximately 69 calories per serving.

Crispy Garlic Fries

Great to serve with burgers or fried oysters.

2 Yukon Gold potatoes, skin on, sliced lengthwise in ½ inch segments
Slice again to make ½ inch potato fingers
6 cloves garlic, minced
4 tablespoons extra virgin olive oil
½ cup fresh thyme leaves

Preheat oven to 400 degrees.
In a large bowl, toss the potatoes with the minced garlic, and oil.
Spread the potatoes in an even layer on a rimmed baking sheet.
Season with freshly ground pepper and sprinkle with thyme.
Roast for about 60 minutes until the potatoes are browned and very crisp.
Crispness depends on size of fries, so check at 45 minutes and after to control roasting for perfect fries.
Serves 4
Approximately 175 calories per serving.

Crispy Garlic Fries

Roasted Butternut Squash with Nutmeg and Cloves
One of our all time favorite side dishes...excellent with Pepper Crusted Halibut.

2 small butternut squash
4 tablespoons unsalted butter
2 tablespoons brown sugar
½ teaspoon nutmeg
2 pinches ground cloves
Olive oil for baking dish

Preheat oven to 400 degrees.
Melt butter and combine it with spices and sugar (reserve).
Cut squash lengthwise. Remove core and seeds.
Place cut-sides down in an oiled shallow baking dish. Bake 30 minutes.
Turn over, brush butter mixture generously over surface.
Continue baking at 400 degrees for 30 minutes or until tender.
Brush with any remaining butter before serving.
Serves 4
Approximately 173 calories per serving.

Puréed Parsnips
Many people have not tried parsnips, but when they do they become raving fans.

3 large parsnips, peeled and sliced into ¼ inch rounds
2 tablespoons unsalted butter
2 tablespoons half and half cream

Boil parsnips at medium high about 7 minutes until easily pierced by a knife. Purée in a food processor with butter and cream.
Add more cream if necessary to achieve a smooth consistency similar to mashed potatoes.
Serves 4
Approximately 133 calories per serving.

Wild Wild Rice with Mushrooms and Sautéed Almonds
A marvelous side dish for the holidays and entertaining.

4 cups low sodium chicken broth (see product page)
½ cup water
1½ cup wild rice, rinsed in cold water
2 tablespoons unsalted butter
2 sweet onions, chopped
Large bunch fresh thyme leaves
4 ounces crimini mushrooms, quartered, stems removed
4 ounces raw almonds, sliced

Bring broth and water to a boil, and then reduce to simmer.
Add wild rice and stir. Cover and simmer 1 hour or until liquid is absorbed.

Caramelize onions in olive oil for 20 minutes at medium heat, stirring frequently. Melt butter in large nonstick skillet at medium heat.
Sauté mushrooms in butter for about 10 minutes.
Set aside. Add a little more butter to the pan and toast almond slices until slightly browned.

Combine onions, butter, mushrooms, thyme and toasted almonds with cooked rice.
Put into oven-proof serving dish.
Wrap and store in the refrigerator. Reheat in oven before serving.
Serves 6
Approximately 274 calories per serving.

Products We Love to Cook With!

We limit the use of processed shelf product because so many are sky high in sodium. *Our favorite brands are listed below…many of them very low in sodium compared to others.* Go to the websites of these incredible products for more information about them.

Pacific Low Sodium Chicken Broth has only 70 mg of sodium per cup, no fat, no carbs, and is very flavorful. It makes recipes using stock much faster to make. This product is available at Fred Meyer and many other stores. Contact manufacturer for stores near you. www.pacificfoods.com

Pomi Chopped Tomatoes from Italy are a delicious natural shortcut for many tomato ingredients, only 20 calories, 10 mg of sodium, no fat, and 4g carbs for half a cup. They have no preservatives or additives. Available on amazon.com. Contact www.pomitomatoes.com for stores near you.

President Crumbled Feta is an easy and very tasty addition to salads or pasta. It is approximately 70 calories per ounce which is a bargain for cheese. It does have 260 mg. of sodium per ounce but typically you don't use very much at one time. It is a natural product made from milk from cows not treated with RBST (hormones). Available at Costco. Contact manufacturer for stores near you. www.presidentcheese.com

Milton's Multi-Grain Crackers are large enough for a piece of cheese or a dollop of spread but they are only 35 calories and 65 mgs of sodium per cracker. They come in several flavors. Our favorite is the Original Multi-Grain, delicious plain or with toppings. Available at Fred Meyer and many other stores. Contact manufacturer for stores near you. www.miltonscrackers.com

La Tourangelle makes a wonderful roasted walnut oil. It's great to have a variety of oils to use in salad dressings. Walnut oil is a delightful variation for salads. It's a California product that borrows the recipe from the 150 year tradition of French walnut oil production. 120 calories per tablespoon, similar to olive oil (no sodium). Available at Whole Foods. Contact the manufacturer for stores near you. www.latourangelle.com

Tandoori Naan Bread is our favorite Naan bread. Fabulous Flatbreads bake their Naan in a traditional tandoori oven where they pick up their smoky flavor. www.fabulousflatbreads.com

Garam Masala is a mainstay of Indian cooking. It is available in Asian and Indian stores. It's a blend of spices: cinnamon, cumin, cloves, coriander, nutmeg and pepper. We use it as a rub for barbecuing skinless, boneless chicken breasts…terrific on the grill! Mix 1 tablespoon each of Garam Masala, chili powder, ground cumin and paprika together. Rub all over the chicken breasts. Cook for 8 minutes each side over indirect heat, lid closed. Check internal temperature. It is done at 175 degrees. Serve with fresh ears of corn cooked over flame on the grill and you have a genuine southwestern barbecue!

Herbs of Provence is a superb addition to your kitchen pantry. It is splendid for seasoning roast turkey or roast chicken. There is a good recipe for the roast turkey on the Williams Sonoma website. It is also excellent in soups and braised dishes. Herbs of Provence are a classic combination of herbs from Provence: thyme, basil, savory, fennel and lavender. It captures the flavors of France like nothing else! 1 oz. size at Williams Sonoma stores or website, 2 ounce refills, at stores only. www.williamssonoma.com

Demi-Glace de Boeuf adds richness and flavor to braised dishes. Great chefs would not be without it! Williams Sonoma has a very good one, intense and flavorful. It's pricey, but because you only use a tablespoon for each recipe, the cost per use is reasonable. It lasts 6 months in the refrigerator after opening. www.williamssonoma.com

Robbins Family Olive Oil and Balsamic Vinegar add so much to salads! If you want to experience one of the world's most exceptional olive oils and the world's best imported balsamic vinegar, try these from Robbins Family Farm. We have never tasted better. They are the *secret* to the perfect caprese salad! You can order these gold medal award winning products directly from the Robbins website. www.robbinsfamilyfarm.com

Our favorite spices, seasonings for Asian recipes are listed below:
Sun Luck Sesame Oil 0% sodium; Sun Luck Chinese Five Spice 0% sodium
Sun Luck Chili Oil 0% sodium; Sun Luck Chili Garlic Sauce 0% sodium
Sun Luck Hoisin Sauce 240mg sodium; Sun Luck Plum Sauce 140mg sodium
Sun Luck Chinese Mustard Powder 0% sodium; Marukan Rice Vinegar 0% sodium
Shiba Mango Chutney 28mg sodium; Sambal Oelek Fresh Chili Paste 110mg sodium
Mae Ploy Sweet Chili Sauce 400mg sodium; JFC Roasted Sesame Seeds 5mg sodium
Kikkoman Less Sodium Soy Sauce (575mg sodium)

Helpful Hints from Our Kitchen to Yours

Access to the chefs…
It's easy! Just e-mail Chef Bob or Chef Ellen at info@fivestarcuisineathome.com. All we need is your name, your e-mail address and where you purchased your book. We will e-mail you a private e-mail address that will enable you to contact us directly if you have a question about any recipe in this book.

Butter…Most of today's great chefs recommend unsalted butter. It is purer and very low in sodium compared to salted butter. We use only unsalted butter in our kitchen.

Cheeses…An assortment of cheeses are essential in the well stocked kitchen. Good cheeses have become very expensive. We suggest buying your cheese at Costco where the downside is you must buy a large piece of cheese, but the upside is you save 50% compared to supermarket prices. Most cheeses, if properly wrapped and stored in the refrigerator, will last a long time. It's worth buying a bigger piece to cut the cost per ounce in half!

Ground turkey…To buy ground turkey, go to a quality market that specializes in organic or natural foods, no additives, no hormones, and vegetable fed. Find one that has a meat department that grinds turkey fresh every day.

How to save money on dried herbs and spices…
Here's how to save money on dried herbs and spices. Buy as much or as little as you need from bulk bins in stores. Many supermarkets and natural food stores offer herbs and spices in bulk at half the price of buying them pre-packaged in jars. Your pantry needs to be stocked with a wide assortment of herbs and spices.

Peppercorns… Pepper is possibly the most important spice in your pantry, truly an essential in cooking today! You will need a good pepper grinder to grind fresh pepper for crusting meats and fish, for omelets, for salads, soups, and the list goes on and on. To keep the cost down, buy peppercorns in bulk and add them to your pepper mill as you need them.

Pots and Pans…See our website for information on the cooking pots and pans, kitchen equipment and timesaving tools we use to create recipes in this book.
www.fivestarcuisineathome.com

Saffron…sets the gold standard for herbs. The price for the best quality Spanish thread saffron is similar to the price of gold…thru the roof! Fortunately you only need to use a few threads in a recipe to get that unique saffron flavor. Even more fortunately, Trader Joe's has a jar of Spanish thread saffron at a very reasonable price. Unfortunately Trader Joe's is not everywhere. If you don't have Trader Joe's in your area, shop around for a local store with saffron at a reasonable price. www.traderjoes.com

Salmon…There is a significant taste difference between fresh salmon and frozen salmon. It's best to wait until salmon is in season and buy it fresh, not previously frozen. You will appreciate it so much more! During the season, Costco offers fresh wild caught salmon filets at very affordable prices. Great for cooking on a cedar or alder plank on your barbie!

Salt…We do not add salt to any of our recipes. You can add salt, but be advised that too much salt is not healthy.* As your palate adjusts to less salt in your food, you acquire a better ability to taste the other unique ingredients, herbs and spices in your food! *Note: Many of today's great chefs recommend kosher sea salt (no additives) rather than ordinary salt.*

*Too much sodium in the body increases demands on the heart, blood vessels, and other vital organs leading to high blood pressure, edema, congestive heart failure, and stroke. Source: CDC (Center for Disease Control & Prevention). Federal guidelines state that a normal body requires no more than 2300 mg of sodium daily, but are now recommending that this ceiling be lowered to 1500 – 1800 mg of sodium daily.

There's nothing quite like fresh herbs…Dried herbs are great in braised dishes and soups, but in salads you really want the taste and flavor of fresh herbs. Unfortunately, they are expensive in the stores. *Here's how to save money on fresh herbs. Grow your own…*it's easy! Just get some pots at the supermarket or plant store, some planting soil, and some herb starter plants at the farmers market. Plant your herbs in April and enjoy fresh oregano, dill, thyme, rosemary, mint, basil, sage, and chives all summer and into the fall.

Vegetables…Plan your menu after you see what is fresh at the market.
Vegetables are infinitely better when they are "just picked." That's why we encourage you to go to your local farmers market for produce and cook whatever is in season! Remember supermarkets need days, sometimes weeks, to get vegetables from the grower to their stores. Vegetables are simply not as good a week or more after they have been picked.

Go to our website at www.fivestarcuisineathome.com for more product tips and helpful hints plus more recipes.

Index

Made in the USA
Charleston, SC
03 December 2009